MORRISON OF WELLINGTON

Photo]   [*Swan Watson, F.R.P.S., Edinburgh*

Geo. H. Morrison

MORRISON
OF WELLINGTON

By
CHRISTINE M. MORRISON

HODDER AND STOUGHTON
LIMITED   LONDON
ST. PAUL'S HOUSE
WARWICK SQUARE
E. C.
4

Made and Printed in Great Britain for Hodder & Stoughton, Limited, by Wyman & Sons Ltd., London, Reading and Fakenham

CONTENTS

THE desire having been expressed by many for a more intimate and personal account of my husband's life and influence than that given in Mr. Gammie's excellent book, " G. H. Morrison, The Man and His Work," I have reluctantly and with much apprehension yielded to the pressure brought to bear on me that I should undertake the task, remembering that not long before he left me, when speaking of Mr. Gammie's forthcoming book, he expressed the hope that, when the real " life " came to be written, I would write it with help.

I have not tried to write a biography, but rather to portray the man in private and public life. The book is sent out with the prayer that many who are at the beginning of their life's work may through it be encouraged and inspired to emulate his singleness of purpose and devotion to duty.

To those who have sent me letters and other material, also to those who have so greatly helped me by their wise counsel and encouragement—but wish to remain unnamed —I desire to express my deep and affectionate gratitude and thanks.

CHRISTINE M. MORRISON

15, College Road,
Dulwich Village, S.E.21.

The following " message " came to me not long after Dr. Morrison died. Who sent it I know not, but it has been the greatest help and inspiration during the writing of this volume :

If I should die, and leave thee here awhile,
Be not as others sore undone, who keep
Long vigil by the silent dust, and weep,
For my sake turn again to life and smile,
Nerving thy heart and trembling hand to do
Something to comfort weaker hearts than thine,
Complete these dear unfinished tasks of mine,
And I perchance may therein comfort you.

INTRODUCTION

SOMEONE has said, and very truly said, that our dear ones are only ours when we have lost them. They have to pass away into the silent land before we know them for what they really are. It is the separating power of things present which dims our vision and prevents our fully seeing and appreciating those who stand immeasurably above us in all high and lofty aims and living.

But when one looks back as from the heights, with a vision that has been purified and made clear through loneliness and suffering, one sees, standing out vividly, the beauties and nobility of a character which, because lived with every day, became so interwoven into the fabric of one's own life that it had to be removed by distance to be fully appreciated.

A true child of nature, and living very near to her heart at all times, Dr. Morrison loved every season as it came round, but, best of all, I think, he loved the autumn with its fulfilment of promise, and the many-hued glory of its riches.

To him it brought no sense of sadness or feeling of finality, rather a sense, as in nature, that after rest and maturing in the hidden depths of God's wondrous love, there would come the great awakening and resurrection of springtime.

To him who lived so near to God, and whose trust in the absolute love and wisdom of the Father-heart was so childlike, autumn was not merely the time of falling leaf and the deadness of approaching winter, but rather a time to buckle on one's armour and go forth in the strength gained in holiday, courageously to face the winter's work.

Had he been allowed to choose his time of going—and sometimes I wonder if God did not really commune with him in these last weeks, because for months past he had been feeling an ever-increasing sense of bodily weariness and oppression, and his talk often turned to our future life—I feel sure he would have chosen to go on the flood-tide of the year.

So all was well for him, and, as I have said elsewhere, " For him there was no sadness in his going, just a short rest after laying down his tools, then a passing through the ever-open door into the eternal springtime in the presence of the Master he had loved so dearly and served so well."

IN MEMORY

(Written by a Member of Wellington Church)

So you are gone ! A gentle, painless passing,
To meet the God you walked with every day,
And in the fuller life—serene and happy—
    Take your appointed way.

God must have had some greater service waiting,
Some work you only could fulfil.
Gone from our hearts the daily inspiration ;
    The voice we loved is still.

We are bereft indeed—a sorrowing people
Walking in darkness ; through a mist of tears
We falter on—yet know for your brave spirit
    Death had no pangs nor fears.

We cannot mourn you long when we remember
Your glowing courage in the darkest hour,
Your radiant faith, and your complete surrender
    Of will, and heart, and power.

In truth for you, no gloom nor grief is fitting,
Your life was love—your very spirit joy.
Gladly you served and taught us—Death can never
    Our fellowship destroy.

October 14th, 1928.

I HAVE been able to glean very little information in regard to his early days beyond what is given in Mr. Gammie's work, but one or two things I have learned from himself, and also from papers which he left to me to be used in the event of his biography being undertaken.

All details of his birth and ancestry, childhood and schooldays, also the period as a student and assistant, have been so fully and skilfully dealt with already, that I have confined my record almost entirely to later days and personal matters.

He was born on the 2nd October, 1866, at 20, Holyrood Crescent, Glasgow, but before he was a year old the family moved to No. 22.

People have often asked me why the doctor was called George Herbert, and many may have wondered whether it was a family name, but I believe that the origin of the name arose from the fact that his mother, " a sweet Highland lady," had been reading

with great pleasure and admiration the poems
of George Herbert just before her baby son
was born, and desired to call him after the
poet.

His mother's death when he was barely
five made a deep impression on him, and the
sense of loss all through his life never left
him. Several times I happened to be in
Callander when he was there, and each time
he took me to see the house in which she
died, telling me how he remembered breaking into violent weeping on seeing the coffin
being carried downstairs, and standing at a
little window on the stairs watching the
train pass which bore it to Glasgow. This
seemed to be one of *the* big things of his
childhood. I think that sense of loss did
three things for him. It made his fatherhood
exquisitely tender. It was as if he said to
his children, " as one whom his mother
comforteth "—" With a mother's comfort I
never knew, will I comfort you."

It produced a certain stillness of soul
which comes from self-discipline, from doing
without. It created a blank which was
never filled, a craving for love which was
neither morbid nor sentimental, but one

which needed all the love which was given him by all who knew him. This need of love was to me one of the most marked features of his character, and I put it down to the fact that he went hungry for the want of it in his childhood. The following, written shortly before he died, bears out what I have said :

" Thank you, dear, for letting me know. The loss of a mother is one of the heaviest this world can bring, and you have my deepest sympathy. You have been blessed above many in having had your mother spared to you so long. I lost mine when I was only five, and I always felt the loss was an irreparable one.

" God bless you, dear girl. I shall not forget you, and Mrs. Morrison joins with me in all.

" Affectionately yours,

" G. H. MORRISON."

Lilybank Gardens,
1928.

Only one other memory of his childhood is to be found, and it comes from one who was his nurse when he was about two years old. Just two weeks before he died, I was speaking at a meeting at Roseneath, on the Gareloch, and at the close was told that an

GEORGE H. MORRISON AGED 9 YEARS

old lady who had been my husband's nurse and had come miles to hear my lecture, would like to speak to me. I found her a dear old person, and of course wonderfully proud of her charge, who had grown up to be so well known, and had actually become Moderator. She had not much to tell me, except that as a tiny boy he was so precocious she was certain he would die young, also that he had loved playing at churches on Sunday, not, Dr. Morrison added, from any sense of prophetic instinct, but because it was the only game his old nurse's conscience would allow him to play on Sunday. Once she went into his mother's room and found him on his knees praying. He was just over two years of age.

Although his mother died at the early age of forty-one, it had always been her fond hope that her youngest son would enter the Church, and this knowledge, as well as the home atmosphere of culture and strong Church interest, and the deep spiritual character of his father, which set its mark indelibly on his son, tended to influence and lead him towards the ministry.

During his university days he passed

through a time of deep spiritual unsettlement, and when he left Gilmorehill, instead of going straight on to the (then) Free Church College, he decided to accept some other work and not commit himself until his mind was absolutely clear that the Church was the true call for him. Fortunately just then, in 1888, he was offered an assistant editorship under Sir James Murray, on the staff of the New English Dictionary at Oxford. This offer greatly appealed to his literary taste and mind, and was gladly accepted. It was during these months in Oxford that he made the great decision in regard to his career.

When the vision came to him, and he was asked what he would have, I think his reply must have been, "Strength to do Thy work." And because he did not ask for success or popularity or even for love, which his nature craved, God gave him all three in addition to the coveted strength. I always felt popularity did not mean much to him, though love meant everything, and surely there never was minister more beloved than he. What was the secret of it ? First, I think, his power to give it, and, second, his

absolute sincerity and simplicity—his friendliness. He never condescended, and the
humblest of us knew it. He radiated friendliness, and even those who never spoke to
him felt its glow.

I have rarely, if ever, met a man so absolutely generous or so essentially lovable.
People meeting him even for a short time,
came under the spell of that generosity of
heart and mind, that rich spending without
a thought of its being anything other than
simply the natural outpouring of a loving
heart upon whomsoever he met who at all
needed it. What an untold wealth of kindness and love he must have sown broadcast
through all those years of his ministry!
The rich harvest of love he reaped came
from the fact that he "sowed seed from his
hand and not from the basket."

His period at Oxford proved most con-
genial to him. I have often heard him say
it was an experience and education he would
not have missed for anything, and would
always be grateful for, as it gave him a sense
of the fitness of words, and a command of
the English language he could never have
acquired otherwise.

B

In 1904, when visiting Oxford together, he took me to call on the Murrays, and Sir James himself took me out to the Scriptorium in the garden where the great work was being carried through, and showed me the desk at which my husband worked, telling me what a wonderfully interested, accurate and eager worker he always was, and what a welcome guest in their home. Sir James ended by telling me the well-known story which Dr. Alexander Whyte never wearied of recalling. Some years after Dr. Morrison left Oxford Dr. Whyte had called to see Sir James Murray, and during their conversation about the dictionary Sir James remarked that his most necessary duty was to make sure that the quotations used were absolutely accurate. "But surely," said Dr. Whyte, "you can trust your contributors, who are all selected men?" "No," replied Sir James, "not one," and then he hesitated and added, "Well, yes, there *is one*, and he is a minister of your own Church." "Might I ask who he is?" asked Dr. Whyte. "Oh, yes," was the immediate reply, "the Rev. George H. Morrison." "He was an old assistant of mine," Dr. Whyte replied with a pride which

he seemed to feel every time he recalled the
incident.

For fifteen months he worked in Oxford,
and then returned to Glasgow, where, from
1889 to 1893 he followed his Divinity course
at the (then) Free Church College, returning
to the Dictionary staff during the vacation
of 1890. A rather unique experience was
the result of this appointment at Oxford.
He was obliged to leave Glasgow before the
Graduation ceremony at which he ought to
have been capped, and it was not until after
he had been minister at Thurso and Dundee,
also Wellington for a few years, that he was
capped for his M.A. degree. I well remember
the day ; the capping took place privately in
the presence of the Senate.

In June, 1913, he received the Degree of
Doctor of Divinity from his Alma Mater.
The Dean of the Faculty of Theology in
presenting him for the degree at the
Graduation said :

" The Reverend George Herbert Morrison
is one of the most popular and successful of
our younger clergymen. Come of a stock
remarkable for the number of able pastors
and preachers whom it has produced, Mr.

Morrison combines in an eminent degree the family gift of instruction with a pulpit eloquence singularly pleasant and attractive. Delightful to listen to, his sermons find willing publishers and a multitude of readers."

During the first year of his Theological course, he had a very serious attack of pneumonia from which recovery at one time seemed impossible. I have a letter beside me from one of his college friends, in which he says : " Intercession was offered for G. H. daily in all the classes, and two of ' The Year ' called daily at his home to inquire for him." However, he made a wonderful recovery, and returned to college in many respects a different man, with a softer voice haunted with a wooing note, a quieter manner, and a more understanding mind. " The cruel fellowship of pain and sorrow had given to him great thoughts of Christ and God, and had deepened his brotherhood, and they left him humble for all his great intellect and fame." Diligently he continued the routine of college work, still reading constantly literature which stood him in good stead in after years,

In the exit he won first place, and almost immediately began a new apprenticeship with Dr. Alexander Whyte, of St. George's, Edinburgh, whose spiritual influence was the greatest G. H. ever experienced. From that pulpit-master he learned much which he held and maintained to the end.

Towards Dr. Whyte my husband always cherished feelings not only of reverence and affection but of the deepest gratitude for all he had been and done for him. The fifteen months spent in St. George's altered his whole life. Up till that time, he had been a student with the haziest ideas of what the real work of the ministry entailed and meant, and to use his own words, " I found an ideal Scottish minister who carried my heart captive. Whatever service I have been able to render in the years that have passed, I owe it entirely to him.

" Think what it must have meant for me, a shy, raw beginner, to live for over a year in close intimacy with such a big soul. His devotion to duty, his dogged adherence to his own work, his mapped out days, his intense love of all good literature, his humility,

his amazing appreciation of the most common-
place service—these things were my school of
pastoral theology.

" Another beautiful thing in his relationship to me was that he would never give me
any advice whatever.   On one occasion, just
before entering St. George's pulpit, I found to
my horror that I had omitted to note the
text for my sermon.   In desperation I turned
to Dr. Whyte for help.   ' Sir,' he replied, as
he walked up and down his vestry, ' I have
enough of trouble to find my own text, without
finding yours.   Now, there is the church
officer, go,' and I went ! "

The following post card is typical of Dr.
Whyte's never failing interest in his old
assistant :

" How you work ! and how proud I am of you !
" Believe me,
" Most warmly yours,
7, *Charlotte Square,*   " A. W."
1913.

The Rev. Hubert L. Simpson, who was
just a child at the time of Dr. Morrison's
assistantship, writes :

" We children in the Sunday School at St. George's,
Edinburgh, were not long in discovering that the

new assistant was different from any other we had
known. Across the intervening years the memory
is vivid of his story about the Ugly Dwarf who had
mysteriously found his way into Mr. Morrison's
study one Christmas Eve. The poor little fellow
was crying because he had the ugliest hands you
ever saw, and his feet were all misshapen. He made
us see the dwarf. And Mr. Morrison said something to him, and he went away. Next Christmas
Eve the Ugly Dwarf came back again. But now
his hands and feet were beautiful, and his face shone
like an angel's. All the year those hands had been
busy doing kind actions, and the feet running
errands of love.

" Those Christmas holidays everybody was re-
telling the story of the Ugly Dwarf. Preaching we
children had listened to, but we had never heard it
on this wise. ' Will it be Mr. Morrison to-day ? '
we would ask, and scamper off to church lest we
should miss anything.

" Long afterwards we learned the secret of that
winsome style and attractive simplicity of utter-
ance. ' —— was the most brilliant of my assistants, but George Morrison was the most industrious
and methodical. I never passed the window of his
room but he was at his desk.' It was his great
master, Dr. Whyte, who spoke. And we saw
another ' tireless hand ' at an Edinburgh window—
not far from Sir Walter's, writing, writing. And
the things that he wrote concerned the King."

Even during these early days of his
assistantship in St. George's, there were

many who regarded him as predestined ulti-
mately to become Dr. Whyte's colleague and
successor, and when for a second time an
increase was being made in his salary, a
request was made that he would not preach
in vacancies. However, he did not comply, as
he said he felt convinced that if he was ever
to do real work in God's service he must
first face the difficulties, problems and bracing atmosphere of some country charge as
well as having more time for study. Seven
months later came the call to Thurso, and
his own first charge.

Professor Grainger Stewart, an office bearer
in St. George's, and one who had ever shown
great interest in the young assistant—asking
him round to his study, where he would go
over his sermon, advising and encouraging in
the kindest and most fatherly way—said to
him when it was decided that he would
accept the call to Thurso : " Mr. Morrison,
you will go north to Thurso and stay there
four or five years, and then come south
again greatly enriched, but whatever you do,
you must never go across the Border." This
admonition must have carried some weight
with Dr. Morrison, because he certainly

never showed any inclination to leave his own country even for a time, although the attention and hope of many vacancy committees in England, Ireland and America focused on him. Many overtures were made to him of which no hint ever reached the outside world, indeed the danger in regard to a London call just the year before he died was past before Wellington heard anything about it, his quoted reason being in the words of the Psalm :

" This is my rest,
Here still I'll stay,
For I do like it well."

Though the only rest he had was the rest he really prized—the rest of the spirit that is stayed on God.

HIS LOVE OF THE " OPEN "

A cousin, Dr. Simpson, of Golspie, one of his closest friends, at my request sends the following :

" I remember very distinctly the morning when the telegram arrived telling of the death of Aunt Lina (George's mother) at Callander. She was much beloved by my mother and my aunt, and it must have made a strong impression on my mind, for I was then only seven years old.

" My mother used to tell me about my grandmother and how she was looked upon as a person to whom the spiritual world was very real, and I have often wondered whether George's spiritual gifts, which were wonderful, had been handed on through his mother. I like to think so, and that reminds me of my mother's brother, the late Dr. H. L. Mackenzie, who for forty years laboured at Swatow, China, as a missionary, and who, during his last leave at home, became Moderator of the Presbyterian Church of England, and was made a D.D. by his Alma Mater, Aberdeen, in recognition of his work abroad. His life is another example of the spiritual tendencies of the Mackenzie family.

" Although George's mother died when he was so young, one could trace all through his life her influence and traits of her character in him.

" There was a well of tenderness in him, of which examples are told. One day an idler set himself to decorate with hat, coat and muffler collected from the cloak-room, the

marble bust in the college corridor of Dr.
William Cunningham, the Disruption leader.
George saw him. 'Please, don't do that,'
he said. 'Why not, George?' 'Because'
—and he blushed—'I don't like it. My
mother used to speak of Cunningham, the
"curly-headed minister," she called him. She
died when I was very young, and that's
about the only thing I remember of her.'"

His visit to the Highlands as Moderator of
the United Free Church three years ago, gave
universal pleasure, and will long be remembered in the places which he found time to
visit. He loved the Highlands, his mother's
country (for she was a sweet-faced and gentle-
voiced Inverness girl), and his last visit gave
us the privilege of recalling the delightful
holidays of our early boyhood spent in
Lochaber and on the Kyle of Sutherland.

His sense of humour was unquenchable,
and sometimes seized him when neither he
nor his friends quite expected it. But it was
always delightful. He loved a good story,
especially a good Highland story drawn from
the heart of the people, and over a quiet
"pipe" in one of his rare leisure hours he
was a charming and an amusing companion.

As some have the gift of an ear for music or an artist's hand and eye, so it seemed to me that as the years rolled on George Morrison had the gift of spiritual insight given to only a few, and this gift he used freely and constantly for others. If ever a man lived for others and not for himself, he was that man. He was faithful to the end, and his reward has come.

All through his life he was a keen lover of the open, and in his young days a clever rock climber, with a sure eye and foot and fearless to a degree that sometimes caused his companions anxiety. The present writer remembers when George Morrison and he, boys of sixteen and eighteen, explored the great eastern rock face of Ben Nevis in search of rare alpine plants. One day we found ourselves picking an Alpine Saxifrage from a dangerous corner on the face of the great precipice. George turned his face towards me, and with a wicked twinkle in his eye said, " What a good thing J—— (naming an anxious relative in Fort William) can't see us just now ! " A few days after this he fell when climbing alone in the same spot, and narrowly escaped fatal injury. He was an accom-

plished botanist, and I well remember envy-
ing him his excellent collection of wild plants.

One holiday spent together was at Fort
William, in the summer of 1882, where I lived
with my uncle and aunt. He arrived armed
with a botanical vasculum and a " spud,"
and told me that we must climb Ben Nevis
together. At that time I was acting as
supernumerary assistant to Mr. Clement
Wragge, the meteorologist who for some years
carried on observations at Fort William low
level station, and also at the top of Ben
Nevis high level station, and at several
intermediary stations, and who latterly
established the Ben Nevis Observatory at
the top of the mountain.

I had made a collection of the alpine flora
of Ben Nevis, of which I was somewhat proud.
My pride had a fall.

I acted as guide for George all over Ben
Nevis, reaching some most inaccessible places
on the precipice face with him. His method
of rock climbing made me feel that he had
come to teach me, for I well remember the
jealous eye with which I watched him
tackle a difficult rock face on the east side
of the " Ben " which I, certainly, would

have been chary of attempting ; but what troubled me most was that within a fortnight, under my personal guidance on the mountain, he had made a collection of alpine flora in every way superior to my best efforts, and what was worse, his plants were properly arranged and scientifically classified under their natural orders, with their scientific and proper names, and mounted in first-class style.

I left Fort William early that season, and returned to work for my degree in Edinburgh, and while there received word from Fort William that George, while climbing alone on the eastern face of Ben Nevis, had accidentally slipped and fallen over twenty feet, mercifully on to a ledge below. He was badly bruised and cut, and rendered unconscious. When he came to himself and looked at his watch, which had stopped some hours earlier, the day was already far spent. He managed with difficulty to drag himself down the 2,500 feet to sea level, and crawled home to Fort William in the evening more dead than alive. He was confined to bed in a rather serious condition for some time, and in his own narrative of the accident says, " This was the only occasion on which I was ever publicly prayed for in church."

When I met him some years later at Oxford, where I paid him a visit, he was assisting in the work of the great Murray Dictionary. I reminded him of our botanical mountain rambles, and he was much amused to know that his scientific knowledge of plants had occasioned me such heart-burning. Incidentally, it taught me more than I ever knew before about them.

Looking back on it all I am quite certain that if he had wished to become a teacher of botany, he could easily have found a Chair of Botany awaiting him in one of the teaching universities.

One of his most treasured possessions, which was never far from his hand, was a copy of Hennedy's " Clydesdale Flora," given to him by his father in 1879, and the tattered condition of the volume told of its constant use.

MANY years ago the Chairman of the Committee in search of a minister to fill the vacant pastorate of the Fifth Avenue Presbyterian Church in New York, asked the Rev. Dr. Douglas Adam, who was just starting on a visit to Scotland, to interview Principal Rainy regarding two well-known Scotsmen.

Dr. Rainy spoke very highly of both men, but told Dr. Adam that, in his judgment, neither was quite suitable for the Fifth Avenue Church. " The man, in my opinion," said Dr. Rainy, " who would be suitable, is one whom the Committee would probably not consider." On being asked " Why ? " Dr. Rainy said : " Because he is at present in a small church, and he has not a great reputation. The man to whom I refer," he continued, " is the Rev. George Morrison, of Thurso."

Thurso, the most northerly town on the mainland of Great Britain, was founded in the twelfth century, and made a Burgh of

Barony in 1633 by Charles the First. Whether the name is of Scandinavian or Celtic origin, opinions differ. The great charm of the town lies, however, in its fine beach and esplanade, and the elevated seaside walk extending eastwards therefrom, with the outlook over Thurso Bay, which possesses a beauty and grandeur unsurpassed on the Scottish coast. Viewed from the esplanade across the bay to the left, a fine sweep of foreshore from which rocky promontories and green slopes rise quickly, culminates in the bold outline of Holborn Head. Northeastwards in the middle distance there rises sheer from the sea, to a height of several hundred feet, the dominating sandstone mass of Dunnet Head. From point to point of these two headlands runs the swift and ofttimes tumultuous Pentland Firth, beyond which on the horizon lies the long stretch of the island of Hoy, its western extremity forming a great bastion 1,100 feet high, looking out to the North Atlantic, its skyline of massive undulating hills gradually decreasing in height till the comparatively low level of its eastern end is lost to sight behind Dunnet Head. Just beyond that lower ground lies

C

the land-locked harbour which from 1914 to 1918 sheltered the Grand Fleet.

Whether under a summer sky with the peaceful waters of the Firth sparkling in sunshine, and the distant Orkneys shimmering and melting into the blue haze of the sky, or in winter when the great billows of the North Atlantic sweep into the bay with awesome majestic stride and crash on the rocky foreshores in great masses of seething foam, the scene is one which never fails in its appeal.

Often has Dr. Morrison spoken both from the pulpit and to his many friends of the inspiration he received from the outlook from his study window over this great panorama.

The following account of Dr. Morrison's trial sermons and early ministry at Thurso is contributed by Mrs. Isabel Cameron, author of " The Doctor," that beautiful character-study of the late Rev. Robert Cowan, of Elgin :

" The bell had ceased ringing. An expectant hush filled the church. Every eye was fixed on the crimson curtain looped back behind the pulpit. At any instant now, our next new candidate might appear in that

curtained opening,* for the pulpit of the
First Free Church, Thurso, was entered from
behind. Going to church in 1894 was a thing
of high adventure. Never did we know whom
we were to have.

" To-day we were especially excited, because the rumour had gone that this young
man was someone especially good ; he was
assistant to Dr. Whyte, in Free St. George's,
Edinburgh ; he was a distinguished scholar,
belonged to a distinguished family.

" Then came the soft sound of the drawn
curtain and we got a glimpse of a raven black
head and a pale face ere he sat down. Still
in tense silence we waited (he prayed) for
our next good look at him.

" A tall, boyish figure, a nobly carried head
but not a boyish face—that was our first
impression. Study and thought had graven
fine lines upon his features, and if taking
away youthful contours had given his face a
sense of latent strength and power. His
hair, jet black, swept upwards from a noble
brow ; before he spoke we knew that our
new ' supply ' was no ordinary man.

---

* One little girl thought that Mr. Morrison came straight
from Heaven through the curtains every Sunday.

"To face a huge congregation as a candidate must surely be one of the cruellest ordeals a young minister can be called upon to endure. Yet if Mr. Morrison was nervous he did not show it. His voice, low and soft, was also perfectly controlled. ' He'll do,' we said with a contented sigh, as we listened to his cultured, restrained tones.

"His first sermon was sufficiently original to be unforgettable. It was ' Two Gardens.' Eden and Gethsemane were contrasted, the world's two great gardens. Like folks in a dream we listened to the old story as if we had never heard it before. The gardens of the world in which were enacted the greatest tragedies of all the ages. It was a solemn sermon, yet it ended on a high hopeful note, and through the darkness of Gethsemane there came to us the shining figure of the Son of God promised from the old days of Eden.

"In those days the second service was at two o'clock, an old custom to enable the country folks to get home in daylight. It must have been hard on the minister though, for it left him little time for rest or preparation. Yet the afternoon service was just as memorable as the forenoon one.

" In the First Free Church there was at this time a large proportion of the congregation who regarded with strong disapproval all changes. And a young man was sure to want changes ; therefore must he be regarded with a certain amount of caution, not to say suspicion. One couple in particular who belonged to this old school were in the church that afternoon. They were facing a very difficult situation because of their private circumstances. It was necessary for them in the evening of their days to pull up old roots and to strike out new ones. Like our national bard they said, ' An' forward though I canna see, I guess and fear.'

" Weighed down with anxiety, they had entered the church with heavy hearts and clouded faces. The text was Joshua's directions to the Israelites when they, too, were facing an unknown path. ' Ye have not passed this way heretofore.'

" A strange and hostile country, the walled city of Jericho to be taken, a warlike army to face and the future all unknown, yet they were bidden to go forward, for God was with them and they were assured of victory. It was a sermon of triumph and

abounding courage. What foe need anyone
fear if God was with them ? What mattered
it if the path was unknown ? He was in
front, leading them to victory.

" Our homeward way that afternoon lay in
the same direction as that of our burdened
friends, and never shall I forget the light
that was in their faces nor how, as they
walked home, they spoke of the courage and
strength which had been put into their
anxious hearts as they, too, faced the way
' they had not passed heretofore.' It was
God's special message to them at that particular time, and I need not say that from
that hour the young minister won them
heart and soul to his side. Had he in the
days to come proposed the wildest innovation
(which he never did) these two faithful hearts
would have followed him loyally.

" By the following August we had our young
minister ' for keeps.' The story of his in-
duction and ordination have been told elsewhere, but no words written or spoken could
do justice to our pride in him. Sunday after
Sunday he poured forth his treasures into our
keeping. He never failed us. He never dis-
appointed us. He never sent us away empty."

A member of his Thurso congregation, now resident in Aberdeen, writes :

" My husband and I were closely associated with Mr. Morrison, as he then was, during his four years' ministry in Thurso, and all our memories of him are of the happiest. My husband was an office bearer, and a teacher in the Sunday School, and I also was a Sabbath School teacher. Sunday was a very strenuous day for Mr. Morrison ; for there were services not only in the forenoon, but in the afternoon as well, and once a month in the evening. In addition, there were services in the country districts in summer, and in winter he held his wonderful Bible Class. But notwithstanding all these services, which must have meant an enormous amount of time and preparation, he generally came down to close the Sabbath School, and speak a few words to the children in his own inimitable way. Sometimes he asked questions bearing on their lesson. I remember he once asked the infant class, ' Who was the writer of the Fourth Gospel ? ' and was gravely informed by one wee mite that it was ' John o' Groat ' !

" One of my very happiest memories is in

connection with a little meeting which was
held in the church hall every Sunday at the
close of Mr. Morrison's Bible Class. It was
intended for young men and women in
lodgings, of whom there were a goodly
number belonging to the congregation. It
was quite an informal gathering, with tea
and friendly talk to set the shy young country
lads and girls at their ease. It was a new
venture, but it was a great success, and
showed the kindness of Mr. Morrison's heart,
and his thoughtfulness for every member of
his flock. It made the church really like a
home. Mr. Morrison did me the great honour
of asking me to make all arrangements and
provide for the tea, and I was only too
pleased to do anything I could to help. I
suggested that he should ask the late Miss
Cowan to be associated with me in the work,
as I knew her heart was in it ; and the two
of us had great pleasure in doing what we
could to make the hall comfortable and
homely. Mr. Morrison provided illustrated
magazines and pictures ; and moved about
among his guests, speaking a kindly word
to each. Then at the end he gathered us
all round the family altar, and commended us

INTERIOR OF FIRST FREE CHURCH, THURSO

to the care of our loving Heavenly Father ; and with a hearty handshake to each we parted, to meet again the following Sunday. Miss Cowan and I considered it a great privilege, and it brought a blessing to our own souls.

" Thurso could not expect to keep a minister of Mr. Morrison's outstanding ability for long, and at the end of four happy and fruitful years, he received and accepted a call to Dundee, to the great sorrow and regret of his Thurso congregation. An amusing story is told of how, after the call to Dundee came, doubt was still felt as to his attitude right up until the day of the Presbytery meeting. When the anxious Commissioners from Dundee reached Thurso an emissary met them at the station with the news : ' He's comin'. He selt his coo yester-day.'

" A day or two before he left, I went up to Castlegreen to say good-bye. His little son, George, had been to church for the first time the Sunday previous, and was full of the wonder of everything—the church itself, the choir, the congregation, his daddy in the pulpit ' preaching to sinners.' The

little man looked up at his father, leaning
against the mantelpiece, and calmly remarked : ' Daddy's a big sinner.' ' No,
no,' said his mother, ' daddy isn't a big
sinner.' ' Oh, but I think I am, my boy,'
said Mr. Morrison with his pleasant laugh.

" On the afternoon of his last day in Thurso,
I saw him pass up Olrig Street alone, and
watched from the windows of our house as
he went along the Victoria Walk. He stood
looking long and earnestly out over the
beautiful bay which he loved so well, as if
to imprint every feature of it on his memory,
and then he slowly retraced his steps home-
wards. Next morning he and his family left
Thurso for Dundee."

The debt that he owed to his four years
in Thurso, he often declared he could never
tell. " Thurso put iron into my blood," he
said. " If any student or probationer wants
to make the most of his life, let him begin
his ministry in Caithness. Of course, I
realise that many things are altered now,
but then the pulpit in the far north was still
a tremendous power. I preached better then
than I have ever done, not because I love

preaching less, but because Caithness loves preaching more, and there one had the enormous advantage of preaching to folk who were thoroughly familiar with their Bible.

"Caithness did not want cold doctrinal preaching, but it did want Biblical preaching, and I have a strong impression that that is what people always do want, although thousands of them do not know it and do not get it.

"The finest compliment I have ever had paid me was by a dear old lady, who viewed everything from the godless south with intense suspicion, and who admitted, after my first communion service, that the 'young man had been divinely preserved from saying anything ridiculous.'"

THE Rev. Robert Wilson, of South Shaw-
lands, who was one of Dr. Morrison's assistants
during his ministry in St. John's, Dundee,
has written this "impression."

At the close of his fine chapter on the
Dundee ministry, Mr. Gammie says that
" perhaps it has been overshadowed, on the
one hand by Thurso with its brilliant
promise, and on the other by Wellington
with its rich fulfilment. Yet," he adds,
" Dundee will always mark a stage, and an
integral stage, in the development of his
career."

That is a just estimate, yet the last sentence requires to be emphasised. Though
the years in St. John's were only four in
number, they were among the happiest and
most pregnant in all Dr. Morrison's life and
ministry. He had had several invitations
to leave Thurso, but had not felt drawn to
any of them. But when the call from
St. John's came he felt, as he said, that it

was in the line of his Master's will for him.
His people at Thurso also felt that St. John's
had behind it a real " call from the Lord,"
and sadly acquiesced. They had resented
previous attempts to attract their young
minister south, and an amusing story is
told concerning one refusal to consider a call.
When it became known that the minister
had declined, one of the elders, when asked
to engage in prayer, gave thanks that " the
minister had chosen rather to suffer affliction
with the people of God than to enjoy the
pleasures of sin for a season."

As a stepping-stone to his great ministry
in Wellington, no sphere could have been
better chosen for him than St. John's. It
was already one of the leading churches of
the city under the noble ministry of Dr.
D. M. Ross, with a splendid body of elders,
and with all branches of work finely equipped.
Yet the note struck by the new ministry,
as Dr. Ross gladly acknowledged, aroused a
new interest and made a fresh appeal to the
heart of the city. Perhaps it might be put
in this way, that the emphasis of Dr. Ross's
message was on the duty of the Christian
man to Christ, while the emphasis of Dr.

Morrison's was on the privilege of the individual in trusting and serving Christ. And to the honour of the elders and people of St. John's let it be said that they discerned that the one was but supplementary to the other, and they gave the new note a hearty welcome. No " traditions " were allowed to stand in the way. The minister was given a free hand. The people heard him gladly, and soon the evening service became crowded with hungry souls from all quarters of the city.

This result was all the more remarkable to those who were privileged to be associated with St. John's at that time, because it appeared so effortless. Hearers left the church wondering what it was that had gripped their hearts. One heard at least a score of personal opinions as to the preacher's " secret." Everything had been so simple, so unsensational, so apparently spontaneous. He had the art, recalls one after many years, of stopping just at a point when you were expecting and wishing him to go on. The same witness probably comes as near the " secret " as any when he says : " He never introduced doubts or difficulties into his sermons, but with his strong faith held steadily on, unresting, unhasting." " I preached what I felt, what I smartingly did feel." These words of Bunyan might be taken as Dr. Morrison's motto as a young preacher to a large city church composed of men and women beset all week with their own doubts and difficulties. He believed that it was a minister's bounden duty to preach only the positive truths that had proved themselves in the experience of his own soul. It was for that reason that, while he was fully abreast of the times as to Biblical criticism and the advances of science on all hands, he resolutely set himself to declare to his people only the sure things of God that were the tried foundations of his own faith.

In the large Bible Class after the evening service it was different. There he never shirked any doubt or difficulty that might be suggested. As in the Round Table in Wellington afterwards, he held himself at the disposal of his young people who were fighting their way to a stronger faith, and many to-day look back to the help and inspiration that came to them as the minister

met them, as they said, on their own ground.
But in the puplit the message invariably
centred on some aspect of the goodness and
mercy of God as revealed in Christ, and the
preacher's one concern was to get the troubled
heart of his people to rest just there. On
one occasion he was told that a certain distinguished and beloved neighbour had ended
a sermon on Amos with the words : " I
have told you what, on the one hand, this
critic says of Amos, and what, on the other
hand, So-and-so holds ; next week I will
tell you what *I* think." The delightful un-
consciousness of the egotism appealed to
Morrison's unfailing sense of humour, and
he laughed hilariously. But after a moment
his face clouded and saddened as he said :
" But what were the poor sheep to *live* on
that week ? "

That question gives his point of view in
all his preaching. At the back of his mind
in all his preparations for the pulpit he
seemed ever to be asking the question :
" What is there here for my people to *live*
on ? " And it was for that reason that he
never found himself able to use a big word
or a technical term which the simplest soul

ST. JOHN'S CHURCH, DUNDEE

in his audience might stumble over. Anyone
listening to him might think that his simplicity of language was artless and spontaneous. Doubtless it became that in the
course of time, but in Thurso and in Dundee
he was still endeavouring to achieve simplicity, and the end he had in view was
that he might give to his people some real
portion of the Bread of Life to live on.
" The proofs of the existence of God have
made many sceptics ; the declaration of the
love of God has made many saints." These
words of the wise Frenchman were demonstrated in Dr. Morrison's Dundee ministry.
One could see them being demonstrated.
In intimate conversations over sermons it
was always evident that the effort of his
mind was towards finding the nearest and
surest road to the mind and heart of the
common man with the message of God's
love. People who heard him often went
away speaking of his "style." As a matter
of fact no one ever troubled less about
style, whether of language or delivery. His
style was truly the man, the man with but
one aim in his heart—to bring men and
women and little children closer to the heart

of their Father in heaven. He read a sermon every day, however busy he might be. Newman, Spurgeon, Ker, Robertson, Maclaren, were taken in rotation. And he did this, not for the sake of learning "style," but, as he said, for his own soul's good, and to see how the great masters got their message home.

It was this desire to get ever closer to the souls of his people that led to his first experiment in extempore preaching. The first taste of freedom from the "paper" came to him at a prayer meeting. He had always had at least very full notes even for that. But one Wednesday afternoon which he had reserved for preparation, was swallowed up by a prolonged visit from a distinguished American. The hour of meeting was drawing near when the visitor left. In something like a panic he prayed for guidance, when there flashed in on his mind the words of St. Paul : "Who, though He was rich yet for your sakes He became poor, that ye through His poverty might be made rich." He confided to his people his own poverty of preparation, and asked them to consider the riches of Christ. For twenty minutes he poured out his soul in the effort to bring home to himself and his hearers the wonder of the love of Christ. For pure eloquence, for rich and varied illustration, and for burning emotion, they had never heard anything like that address, and one can still recall how the people went out awed with a joy unspeakable.

For a considerable time he looked back on that experience as pointing the way to a nearer approach to his people. He hesitated, however, to attempt extempore preaching on the Sabbath. One night, after evening service, as he walked home very gloomily with his assistant, he expressed great disappointment with the day's work. He said he had had two well-prepared and fully written sermons, but that he felt he had entirely failed to reach his people. The assistant, recalling the triumph of the prayer meeting, ventured to suggest that he might try the experiment at a Sabbath service. The suggestion was received in silence, but on parting that night he said : " Well, brother, if I make a fool of myself next Sabbath morning you will be to blame." Next Sabbath morning saw a great triumph. The people were completely taken by storm. Though his evening sermon was a written one, the " paper " was no longer master but servant, and that night he walked home on air, chuckling again and again, and saying, " Yes, that's preaching."

We have said enough to show that the Dundee ministry was indeed " an integral stage in the development of his career " as a preacher to a large and varied city congregation. The same may be said of the development of his career as a great pastor. Dundee as a city has much in common with Glasgow. Its people have much of the same open-heartedness and open-handedness as the people of the western city. St. John's was not unlike Wellington in its office-bearership and in the types of its members. Though not so large in numbers, it was still a large congregation, with varied needs that demanded the full strength of a minister in the way of visitation. It was in Dundee that Dr. Morrison developed his system of getting round his people regularly. His visits were very brief except in special cases, but though short in time, they left behind them a trail of affection and sympathy. He appeared to have the power of never seeming to be hur-

ried in his calls and yet of packing into each
a wondrous amount of interest. He did not
"take worship" in every home, but only where
illness or some family difficulty or problem of
the heart called for it, yet the impression
left was always that of a true man of God.
With the sick and the aged he kept in constant touch, taking a sort of boyish delight
in giving them surprises, either in person or
by his quaint messages.

It was in Dundee also that Dr. Morrison
put into full operation his method of co-
operation with his elders. He had a great
ideal of the Scottish eldership, regarding
them with all honour as ordained to be over-
seers, with the minister, of the flock of Christ.
No finer tribute to Dr. Morrison's attitude
towards his elders could be given than that
of Mr. Mackie Smith, the esteemed Session-
Clerk of St. John's : " To be associated with
him as an elder was a great privilege and a
very happy memory. His graciousness and
gratefulness for any help given were always
noticeable, whilst his whole-hearted devotion
to the spiritual well-being of his congregation
was an inspiration." The following extract
from an ordination address to new elders

gives Dr. Morrison's conception of the place
of an elder in a congregation. It might be
taken as an ideal for all elders and pastors :
" In accordance with old Scottish custom,
you will be set apart to separate districts.
And if you only knew how clearly the blindest
minister detects the impress of the elder in
his district, and if you only thought with
what appalling clearness that impress must
be evident to God, it would lead you, brethren,
to a fresh consecration and a more earnest
cry for light and guidance. Come to your
district as a friend and equal. Give it your
heart, your help, your purse, your prayer.
Do not lose patience with that careless
family. *Devise ingenious ways of being kind.*
Let folk be so sure that 'you are thinking
of them that their thoughts will naturally
turn to you in trouble." Mr. Mackie Smith,
who furnishes this extract, truly says that
" we seem to have in it a rule for the ordering
of his own ministry." He asked of each elder
in his own district to put into practice the
ideal he set for himself as pastor of the whole
congregation. His great namesake, George
Herbert, suggested that the Christian man
should ever be ready to welcome any tempta-

tion to do kindly things that offers itself.
George Herbert Morrison put it positively
for his elders as for himself: " Devise ingenious ways of being kind." To their
honour, be it said, that his elders in St. John's
rose nobly to his ideal. And it was that
ideal that was carried forward to Wellington
and became, in great part, the secret of that
amazing knowledge of the families and in-
dividuals of that huge congregation which
became the envy of all his brethren. His
elders were his eager and affectionate remem-
brancers.

With all his activities in the pulpit and in
the homes of his people he was making
his name known to a wider public by his
pen. His inimitable articles in the *British
Weekly* made every Sunday school teacher
in Scotland his debtor, and by their devotional worth made that excellent journal a
friend and Sunday companion in countless
homes. These articles were written on Tuesday forenoons, for he had the power of re-
deeming his hours. His monumental edition
of Boston issued from Dundee. He made
its preparation a sort of recreation, trudging
round the Boston country with his friend and

elder, Mr. Colin Sharpe, gathering the local colour, and delighting his companion by his intimate knowledge of plant and flower. From Dundee also came his first great volume of sermons, " Flood-Tide," which was destined to be the first of that wonderful series of volumes that set him in the true succession of great British sermon-writers.

Dr. Morrison's wonderful " way " with children was learned in his own happy home in Windsor Street. No one could be such a child among children as he was among his. One recalls an occasion when father, mother, and children were surprised on their hands and knees on different parts of the study floor, round the whole circumference of which was stretched a railway track, while a steam engine made its way along to the delight of all. It was a birthday present from Dr. Alexander Whyte to Sandy, who was named after him. The minister's power of entering and sharing the joy of it all was a delight to see, and it was pleasant also to think of the touch of the child in the great minister of St. George's that led him to go out and purchase that wonderful engine for the wee son of the man on whom his mantle was falling, though he was to wear it with a difference.

We see not to the close. That happy little scene in the Manse at Dundee was enacted only a few short months before the summons came from Glasgow. And he was destined to carry with him to Wellington an even richer spiritual equipment than that great congregation had looked for—the spiritual equipment of a great sorrow worthily borne.

DR. MORRISON commenced his ministry in Wellington Church, Glasgow, on May 13th, 1902, in his thirty-sixth year, and the eighth year of his ordained ministry. He used to say smilingly that he must have been pre-ordained to be Minister of Wellington, although when a student at the university he, a staunch Free Churchman, used to look with wonder, but no special interest, on the massive U.P. Kirk with its great pillars and commanding site opposite the university, that was slowly reaching completion, little dreaming that ere twenty years had gone he would stand in her pulpit as minister of that great and historic congregation.

That ministry, which began on a date and in a month which might by superstitious folk be considered unlucky, lasted without a break, except for two absences caused by severe illness and his Moderatorship, till the time of his death in October, 1928.

Beginning his ministry at that season

which I might say typifies the time of fresh
and full beauty, new outlook, and hopes and
aspirations, it seems very beautiful and
significant to me that his last sermon in
Wellington should be preached on Harvest
Thanksgiving Day, and that the text chosen
was, " Cast thy bread upon the waters ;
for thou shalt find it after many days." To
many who were present that night must
remain indelibly printed on their minds the
picture of him as he stood there in the dim,
quiet church, surrounded by the rich glowing
mass of autumn foliage, flowers and fruit, all
lighted by the golden glow from the hanging
lamp overhead, while he pleaded earnestly
with his hearers to sow lavishly of their
finest for the Master's sake, strong in the
hope that when harvest came they would
reap abundantly.

Born and bred in Glasgow—one to whom
her very dust was dear—he returned from
Thurso and Dundee to the West, knowing
full well what life in his native town meant,
as he described it " a very eager earnest
free thing." He had a very great admiration for Glasgow business men of the
best type, and I often heard him say, " I

have a session that it would be hard to beat."

I need not dwell on the rich and joyous fullness of his ministry in Wellington, or on the deep affection and harmony that characterised the relations between minister and people, but I may say that he loved his people with a devotion, consecration and loyalty that never wavered, and that his constant prayer and desire was for their highest happiness and spiritual welfare.

In the following chapters I have tried—as I have been asked—to give a simple, true and intimate picture of the man as I saw and knew him in the home and at his work.

Punctual and methodical in everything he did, his usual routine when at home was to rise as the University clock struck seven-thirty. Breakfast was at eight-fifteen, and before he sat down to that meal he had fed the waiting birds in the garden and the cats, which were always awaiting him in the breakfast-room.

During breakfast, if we were alone, he read through the births, deaths, University passes,

in the daily paper, then opened his correspondence, putting in the waste-paper basket, which
stood at his left side, all useless material and
on a chair at his right all letters and papers
to be answered or kept.

Prayers came immediately after breakfast,
and then he went to a writing-table in the
window and before leaving the dining-room
he had replied to every letter that required
an immediate answer, and had also sent post
cards of congratulation to the parents of any
new babies, or to young people who had
passed examinations. Also, if he had received news from anyone abroad, he sent a
card to their relatives telling them of the
fact. All correspondence not of urgency was
laid aside to be answered later by himself or
secretary. This was his daily custom and
one of the reasons why he rarely got behind-
hand or overwhelmed. Every type of letter
and paper was carefully filed and kept, also
every paper relative to engagements, until
after the engagement was fulfilled. I frequently saw the absolute necessity for this,
as some people seemed to have a very
haphazard way of booking engagement
dates, and on several occasions awkward

complications were averted ; as, for instance,
when he was advertised to preach in a London
church a week too soon, but was able to show by
correspondence that the error was not on his
side.   Only twice do I remember him making
serious mistakes in regard to his engagements ;
once when he forgot to enter a marriage in
his diary, and was only reminded of it when
the car arrived at the manse to take him to
the ceremony ; the other, during his moderatorial year, when he made two engagements
for one evening, and I had on short notice to
take his place at the opening of an Evangelistic Conference.   It was my first appearance in a pulpit as a preacher, and I cannot
express what my feelings were when I followed
the minister up the pulpit steps, and faced a
huge congregation gathered to listen to the
Moderator.

His prompt courtesy in regard to answering any invitation received was most noticeable.   As a rule the reply was sent by
return of post, but if, as sometimes happened,
the duty was passed on to me, it was invariably accompanied by the injunction,
" Now, see and do not forget to reply to this
at once."

Immediately after having dealt with urgent correspondence he retired to his study (except in summer when he generally spent a little time in the garden), and from then on until lunch at one-thirty, he worked steadily, and if possible, without interruption.

I thought I knew something of the endless detail and thought brought into his everyday work, but to me it has been a revelation, through correspondence and information sent in, in connection with this record of his ministry and home life, to learn how much was accomplished far beyond all that came to my knowledge. He certainly did not let his left hand know what his right was doing, and there must be countless numbers who bless his memory to-day.

Looking back, I just fail to understand how he accomplished all he did in regard to writing and studying, because his people were never allowed to feel neglected, no matter how much extra work came to him, and as a rule he visited every afternoon for several hours.

He kept an accurate account of every visit paid, and the last year he lived, in spite of many extra claims on his time, his book

showed a record of over twelve hundred
pastoral calls. His district books, with the
names of every member and adherent (also
the children with necessary details) were
kept in perfect order and up to date. For
several years before his death he adopted
the card index system as well, so that within
a few moments he could ascertain the name,
address, or particulars of any of his 1,868
members — these members being exclusive
of the mission church members, who numbered several hundreds.

I also know that unless some outside
interruption came, his sermons were finished
and written out by midday on Friday, and
that he rarely worked on them during the
afternoon or evening. I do not remember
him ever saying, " My brain won't work "
or " The sermon won't come," but sometimes
he would appear at lunch-time on a Friday
with his face very flushed, and looking fagged
but triumphant, and he would remark, " I
think I have got something good for my
bairns on Sunday." That was the only information in regard to his work that he ever
gave, but these days I knew that writing
had not been so effortless as usual.

Photo]   [*Annan, Glasgow*

DR. MORRISON WHEN HE WENT TO WELLINGTON

Dr. H. Sloane Coffin, of New York, writes :

" I spent a memorable week in February, 1926,
with Dr. Morrison in his home, where he had graciously invited me to stay while I was delivering
the Warrack Lectures in Glasgow. I was at once
impressed with his amazing industry. Each day
he carried through an immense programme of study,
writing, visiting and Church business. He worked
with system. He would arrive punctually at the
breakfast table, glance through the morning newspaper, conduct family worship, and the moment
breakfast was over start in upon a thoroughly
ordered day. He appeared to have not only a
time to begin each task, but also a time when he
expected to finish it. One morning each week was
set apart for the article which he contributed during
many years to the *British Weekly*. He did not
seem at a loss for a theme. The fecundity of his
mind was astonishing. He would set himself to
outline his thought, and then write off the article
all at one sitting. His sermons were prepared in
the same methodical manner. He had acquired an
art of composition, and all his public utterances,
both in content and style, were constantly on the
same high level.

" I had known him by his books, and had thought
of him as dowered with keen spiritual insight, a
potent imagination, a poetic touch and a genius
for opening up the riches of the Bible.

" I was surprised to find him a man of first-rate
administrative ability. He not only managed his
time, but he managed the arrangements of a large
congregation with deft skill. He had a grasp of

E

affairs and took his part with distinction and force in many institutions in the city and in the life of the United Free Church."

By lunch-time one found that a morning's stint of creative work had been accomplished. Then the afternoon was devoted to pastoral visitation, upon which he would go with both a list of members in a given district and a list of special cases—folk in sickness or sorrow or some other need. By wise management of his time he succeeded in overtaking a large number of calls in an afternoon. Sometimes he would manage to return half an hour before dinner-time and slip into his study, where behind a closed door he would tear the essential message out of some book or article, or prepare himself for some occasional address to be delivered that evening.

After dinner, if there was no church service or meeting, he almost invariably had callers till ten or ten-thirty. Then, after having written up his notes for the day, came the precious quiet hour with pipe and book till midnight. Really free evenings were few and far between, but a wondrous treat when they did arrive.

He refused absolutely to answer any telephone calls after 9.30 a.m. unless it chanced
to be a call of real urgency, and oft and many
were the calls and messages I had to answer
and the importunate people I had to stave
off. I know I was not always loved when
I was at the telephone, but that is one of
a minister's wife's most difficult duties—
trying to make people realise that it is not
the length of time they keep him but the
breaking of the continuity of thought that
really matters—and the "Can't-I-speak-to-
him-for-just-one-minute" folk are as serious
a menace to a minister's work as those who
would call on a Saturday forenoon and look
astonished and hurt when told they could
not see him at all. It was only by keeping
the morning hours sacred to study every
day in the week that he managed to keep
level with his great task, and go into the
pulpit on Sundays with a fresh message well
prepared for his people.

Of course there came at intervals morning
interruptions such as funerals or meetings,
and these he met with his usual unruffled
calm. I can truthfully say that in twenty-
five years I never heard him make one

complaint or grumble when the call to duty came, even when it meant postponing or putting off long-made plans, or breaking into holidays. His faithfulness to every call—no matter what the hour of day or night might be (and frequently he was called out very late at night)—was a source of constant wonder to me.

Many people thought, and said, that he took too little part in the public and administrative affairs of the church work, but they did not know how courageously and cheerfully he worked, handicapped almost constantly by digestive trouble which caused him extreme discomfort and often severe pain. He never complained, nor would he accept sympathy, but he knew his own limitations, knew how far his strength would carry him, so he concentrated all his powers on the work that lay to his hand in Wellington. Who, looking on his work there during twenty-seven years as preacher and pastor, will not admit that he knew best ? Self-advertisement was so abhorrent to him that people never knew how many honouring invitations he received (and refused) from all over the world.

Invitations came from many important and influential churches, either asking him to become their minister, or to preach for a stated time ; or requests that he should undertake lecture tours in America, Canada, or Australia. I can remember at least four different Chairs at home and in the States that he was invited to occupy.

All these requests he considered prayerfully, then quietly turned down. To stand in high places or to gain notoriety made no appeal to his simple mind, and nothing made him more angry than when the word " popularity " was applied to himself or to his ministry.

His one deep desire was to spend, and be spent, in the service of Christ so that he might be an influence for the highest and best, in the civic and church life of the city he loved so well.

His passionate love for the city of his birth and all that pertained to her welfare was one of the outstanding characteristics of the man, and he always said it would take a very strong force to move him from Wellington and Glasgow. The truth of these assertions was shown in the light of many attempts that were made throughout his ministry.

As someone truly has said : " He did not dig many channels, but the one he dug was very deep."

Few realised how his sensitive nature suffered on account of the non-carrying power of his voice, the result of a serious illness in his student days, or how the fear that he would not be heard made him refuse many invitations to speak and preach in untried buildings.

He was rarely if ever nervous about any public appearance, because nothing was ever left to chance and he was always carefully prepared ; but I know how the dread of not being well heard shadowed his biggest hours, and made him concentrate more and more on his own congregation and its work, where he was loved and the people were accustomed to his voice.

In spite of this disability, and the fact that some complained of being unable to hear him distinctly, the crowds that flocked to Wellington never lessened. This comforted his heart, and he used to remark whimsically : " They don't come to admire me, so some of them must hear me." His voice, though low-pitched and not strong, was a perfectly trained voice. He knew it could only carry by the greatest attention to its compass, and it had a haunting quietness that brought peace and comfort to many a troubled heart.

"In St. John's, Dundee, which during his ministry was acoustically one of the worst churches in Scotland for a voice such as his, there were many of the somewhat deaf and those who sat in the back pews who had the utmost difficulty in catching the whole of his sermons, yet, strange to say, these very people were soon the most enthusiastic among his listeners and admirers."

A delightful and significant incident occurred when the news spread that Wellington Church, Glasgow, had again approached their minister, and it was probable that he would accept the call.

The whole body of office-bearers, elders and deacons waited on the minister at the manse to give him an overwhelming impression of their desire that he should stay with them. After hearing their plea and telling them how much touched he was by their presence

and words, he said that in all frankness he
ought to tell them that he knew he was
not well heard in St. John's, and that it
might be well for them to have a preacher
with a stronger voice. Thereupon came the
assurance from all sides, " We hear you fine,
Mr. Morrison ; we hear you fine," and from
one of the oldest and best-loved elders, to
whom the Doric was dear, came this beautiful
tribute : " It's like this, ye see, we would
rather hear a' we dae, frae Mister Morrison,
than hear a' we would hear frae onybody else.
An' that settles it, I'm thinkin'." His method
was not earthquake, wind or fire, but the
voice of gentle stillness, and it conquered
many who might have resisted more clamorous
methods.

An invitation which came to him in 1922,
but which he felt obliged to refuse, was from
the College Committee of the United Free
Church, offering him the appointment of
Warrack Lecturer on Preaching, in the three
colleges of the Church. The invitation appealed much to his mind, but, as I have
said, he knew his limitations, and his own
work must not suffer.

Scarcely a year passed without his re-

WELLINGTON CHURCH, GLASGOW

ceiving invitations to preach in America and
Canada, but he consistently refused all overtures, never taking preaching engagements
during his holidays, as he always said his
own congregations had first claim on the
best he could give. However, after his tour
in South Africa such kind and insistent
letters came from both the United States
and Canada, beseeching him to consider a
two months' spring visit, that he had practically settled that we should go in 1929.
However, ere then came the call which
cannot be ignored, and he journeyed to that
land from which there is no returning.

A favourite saying of his, and one which
he carried out to the letter in his daily life,
was " Do it now." Had he not followed
this motto closely he could never have carried
through the work that was hourly accumu-
lating.

He had a place for everything in his mind,
and this characteristic showed in his work
and daily habits. He had one peculiar trick
which always intrigued people. Generally
after a long afternoon of visiting he would
come home with several knots tied in his
handkerchief. These were to remind him of

requests, promises or incidents met with during his afternoon's visiting, and he would go straight into his study, before removing his hat, and untie the knots after having taken notes of their significance.

One noticed his neatness. His study was a miracle of tidiness and his desk did not betray a disorderly sheet of paper. It was indicative of the man's mind. He left nothing in his sentences or in his congregation's affairs at loose ends.

He knew where to lay his hand on every book and paper without a moment's delay. He rarely sat at his big desk when really working, but in an upright chair by the fire, and by his side stood a small table to hold necessary papers and books. He had also a high-standing desk, where all books of reference, dictionaries, etc., stood. At the end of the study there was a tall cupboard— made to his own design—and here all writing materials, ink, blotting-paper, etc., were kept. The lower part was divided into drawers of different sizes, and in them was stored all his sermon and other manuscript, each with the number of times preached, and the place and date marked on it. The study at all times was a haven of order, peace and comfort. There was always a large coal fire burning, and flowers in abundance, and to many, in that quiet room there came peace of heart and mind, conviction after wavering doubt, and fresh courage and determination to begin anew. He loved that study, and before a holiday was half over would be wearying to get back to it and his books.

There is no day of rest in a minister's week, Sunday least of all, and Dr. Morrison's Sundays were full and taxing to a degree. He rose and breakfasted at the usual time, the only difference in the routine being that the reading at worship was omitted and only a prayer of intercession for blessing on the day's work was offered. From nine till ten-thirty he was in his study, then he walked very leisurely up the hill to the church, arriving there about ten minutes before the hour of service.

Extract of letter from Rev. Stuart Parker, Toronto :

" Dr. Morrison was in the truest sense a Good Man ; he had the gift of a great love in himself, and of awakening a corresponding love in others. I have no words to tell you how he impressed me.

People talked about his sermons. I did not hear many of them ; but above all such attempts at self-expression there was to me the man himself—inexpressible unless by personal contact—and he was to me the embodiment of sincerity and kindliness. So much did he grow upon me, while I was in Belmont Church, that I counted it a blank Sunday if I did not meet him on the hill and have a word with him before going into church. He may not have been conscious of the extent to which I leaned upon him. But I did lean upon him, and looked forward week by week to those few words we exchanged about our sermons every Sunday morning. I felt somehow that he was friendly and kind to me—a mere beginner in the work of the church—and his invariable encouragement, ' See you tell it straightly and simply to them ! ' was my weekly thrill. Surely God has an honourable place in the Kingdom for Dr. Morrison. A thousand men have taken his sermons and used his ideas. I never did. But I have used his inspiration. I have always tried to think of him as one who translated his extensive scholarship into the language of common folk, and have tried in the case of my own limited scholarship to do likewise."

An Australian's impression of a service at Wellington :

" The thing which struck us was the way the Scottish people worship. If ever you go to Glasgow go to the Wellington United Free Church right under the shadow of the University, if you wish to see what I mean. Dr. George H. Morrison is the minister. I can safely say that I was never more moved by congregational worship than I was in this great church. I discovered that the organist was blind, but I soon realised that his soul had eyes, and through these eyes he sees things which he translates into music. I would not have cared if there had been no sermon at all, I was so carried away by the Scottish worship. Every one sings, and, what is more, you cannot stand there and not sing. And while they sang I was far away on the wild, heather-covered mountains listening to the Covenanters singing the same Psalms while they held their swords ready for battle. I understood why it was that the Scots of to-day know how to sing the Psalms. They never remembered learning them, but through generations they have sung them, and the experience of the past has put such a reality into the words, that every Psalm is a battle chant.

" There was no collection to break in on the service—that is taken at the entrance doors ; there were no notices to jar and confuse (I wish I knew how they let the people know of the meetings) ; every pew was a ' Let ' sitting, and yet when you ask the elder at the door, ' Would you kindly show me a seat ? ' he smiles and says, ' Sit just wherever you please.' and you find that the hundreds of visitors are doing this, and all seemed welcome to seats and books, and the smile of the seat-holders when they came along. My trip to Scotland put new heart into me. If some of the churches farther south are empty, I can only say the churches which

I saw in the north were packed with reverent crowds. Here is a question for you to answer. Do you think that the fact of such worship on the Sabbath has anything to do with the unfailing courtesy during the other six days of the week? If so, then their weekly actions are daily acts of worship. No wonder the public and united worship on the Sabbath is so beautiful, for the Sabbath reacts on the weekday, and the weekday reacts on the Sabbath."

No one was allowed to enter the vestry before service (unless on a matter of extreme urgency) except Mr. Turner, the organist.

The last few moments before service—perhaps among the most solemn and sacred in a minister's life—were spent alone, and when he entered the church there was always a look of quiet calm and strength on his face as if he had come straight from the Presence.

The friendship, understanding and sympathy between Dr. Morrison and Mr. Turner through all the years was a very strong bond, and I shall allow him in his own words, taken from his speech on the occasion of Mr. Turner's semi-jubilee, as organist in Wellington to testify to this.

DR. MORRISON'S APPRECIATION OF
MR. TURNER

" If I were to try to analyse, just a little, this
long fellowship, if I were to try to analyse, just a
little, our sources of gratitude to Mr. Turner, I
should, without the least hesitation, put in the first
place his spiritual interpretation of praise in the
services of the Lord's Day. I go a good deal about the
country preaching, as you know, and with the fullest
conviction I say this, Heaven help the Church, Heaven
help the minister, when the organist is out to be
brilliant, to assert himself ; it is fatal, no matter
what his gifts are, and all through these long years
Mr. Turner has realised that he and the pulpit have
been working together for one spiritual aim, and
that is the help of man and the glory of God.

" I get a great many letters, I am glad and proud
to say, from all kinds of people, expressing their
gratitude as to what Wellington has meant to them,
and it would surprise you to know in how many of
these letters Mr. Turner's name comes in. Here is a
letter which arrived two nights ago ; I am not
going to read it, it is a long letter, but just listen
to this. The writer is a Glasgow business man,
not a member of the church, a man who at one
time found it a little difficult just to keep in the
old right paths, and this is what he says : ' I can
never forget that Mr. Turner's music, along with
your words of comfort and hope, have saved many
a poor erring sinner like me, and helped to restore
him to the faith of his fathers.' Now, ladies and
gentlemen, just imagine for a minute if the writer

had said this, ' I cannot tell you how much I have enjoyed the brilliant music of Mr. Turner.' Don't you see, at once the whole atmosphere of Wellington would have been different.

" There are few minutes in a minister's life more solemn and sacred than the few minutes before he goes into the pulpit to preach the everlasting gospel. If he is a wise minister, and if he has got a wise church officer, as I have, he will be very careful to see that the door of the vestry is kept strictly shut. There is only one man who has the right to be there, and he must be there, and that is the organist, and, mark you, if the organist is un-spiritual, if he is foolish, if he is a talkative kind of creature, the strain becomes intolerable. And I should like to take this opportunity of bearing witness that through all these long years, in these quiet moments before preaching, the presence of Mr. Turner has always made it easier for me to go into the pulpit. I sometimes think how deadly tired Mr. Turner must be of listening to me as he has been doing for three and twenty years, and then do you know how I comfort my heart ? I begin to think that for nearly three and twenty years I have been listening to him, every Sunday, every meeting, listening to him, and I can say truly, that so far from being tired of him, I view his gifts with greater admiration to-night than I think I ever did in the past."

Another proof of his great appreciation and regard for Mr. Turner found expression in 1915, when he dedicated his volume " The Wind on the Heath" with the following graceful tribute.

To Fred Turner, Esq., Organist, Wellington Church.

DEAR MR. TURNER,

" I should like to inscribe this volume to you in token of our happy comradeship in service now extending over many years. You have often been good enough to tell me that you have been helped along the way by the message from the pulpit. I can as truly say that my ministry would have been vastly different without the aid of our service of praise which you have always led and interpreted with such skill and reverence and beauty. That you may be long spared, rich in the esteem of all who know you, to carry on your labour of love, is the sincere wish of

" Yours most truly,

" GEO. H. MORRISON."

Mr. Turner says :

" The last Sunday evening that Dr. Morrison preached in Wellington he came into the vestry where I was standing before the fire and said to me : ' I should like to have your portrait painted just as you are now. I meet you just with the same pleasure as I did twenty-six years ago.' I replied (in all sincerity) : ' I feel just the same,' and added, ' I hope you will be here all my time, as I do not wish to start working with another man.' His humorous reply was, ' Ditto with dots ' ! "

How little did either realise that never again would they meet and hold friendly converse in that quiet vestry, hallowed for them both by such countless precious and sacred memories.

F

THERE is no real need to describe the activities of Wellington, or the part the Doctor took in them. The usual agencies were to be found, but to everything he brought the distinguishing touch. His outlook, however, found expression in some special features, which show the universality of his interests.

Perhaps the most outstanding feature of his ministry was the experiment he made a few years after he came to Glasgow, of inviting well known and distinguished preachers from all countries to occupy Wellington pulpit during July and August, the real holiday months in Glasgow. He undertook this venture with the hearty co-operation of his office-bearers, and it turned out to be one of the greatest blessings of his ministry, many of his brethren in his own and other denominations following his example. These holiday services caused quite a revolution in the summer church life of Glasgow and the huge attendances showed how much they were appreciated.

His June lectures, which were held on four Monday evenings, were looked forward to year by year by hundreds of people, including students of Bible Criticism, and as the Doctor revelled in this kind of work, and put his whole heart and mind into it, these lectures became a recognised feature to Christian workers of all denominations.

The third special feature of his ministry was, I think, the " Round Table," and it has been dealt with elsewhere. It was a piece of work very dear to his heart and peculiarly his own, and at it his genius as a teacher and leader was singularly noticeable.

SUNDAY EVENING SERVICE

During the twenty-five years that I sat in the Manse pew in Wellington I had ample time and opportunity to watch and wonder at the crowds that came with almost never varying regularity to the evening services. Any charm of novelty must long since have passed away, and yet his power of attraction held to the very end. Queues were to be found outside the church as regularly as

Sunday evening came round, and if one went late it was to find every inch of accommodation taken up, and even in the Manse pew one learned what it meant to be tightly packed together. Sometimes I had to vacate my place and go into the choir. The evening congregation was always an interesting study. All ages were represented, but young men and women composed the larger part of the audience. Watching the rapt, upturned faces of the listeners during the sermon, one felt that they were different from the ordinary " popular " audience. There was about them a thoughtfulness, and on some faces a look as of wistful yearning after the things that really matter. They were certainly not drawn or attracted to Wellington by any sensationalism or adornment in the form of service, which was absolutely Presbyterian in its severe simplicity—a form that the Doctor ever strove to maintain.

Every minister is proud to wear the hoods he has honourably won, but there was one instance of Dr. Morrison's consideration for the feelings of others, and unselfishness, which I think is known to very few. Except on special occasions, and at marriages, he never wore a hood. Learning that to some of the older members of Wellington, who were very conservative, the wearing of the hood would really cause distress of mind, he decided, without a murmur, to appear at all the usual services without it. Personally I always regretted this, as the hood gives an added dignity to the preacher, and is, after all, only an outward token of achievement.

Watching those young people—gathered from all ranks of society and with so many and varied wants and needs—one felt that here, in this quiet place to which they had been drawn, they were finding what they had come seeking and what was essential. Because the Doctor preached Christ, he did not merely illustrate his theme from the Christian story—Christ *was* his theme. Through his great love for humanity and his broad-mindedness he had acquired the wonderful gift of making contact with every type of character, and men and women burdened and perplexed, felt his understanding and sympathy, and gathered round him, as in olden days at eventide they gathered round Christ and were healed and comforted. Most of his evening sermons were addressed to young men and women, and what an insight into the spiritual trials and difficulties of young people he had !

Some years ago a well-known writer said : " Dr. Morrison has long been the despair of many who have tried to wrest the secret of his success from his preaching, notably from his famous Sunday evening addresses, with their grey and silver enchantment."

These words were true up to the end. There was something intangible about the power—something that it was impossible to describe in words—but the power was there, and it could be, and was, felt. When asked about his secret, as he often was, he would reply : " I don't know anything about a secret. I simply get my message, then I prepare my heart and mind to deliver it, sit down and write it, and on Sunday I give it to my people." He was no orator in the accepted sense, but he carried faith and peace with him to the pulpit, which conveyed to his listeners a sense of stillness and calm, so that they felt that they were brought into the secret place of rest and quiet joy through him. Now that he has passed beyond the veil, there are many who will look back on

these quiet Sunday evening hours and recall
the haunting sweetness of the Doctor's voice
gently pleading with them to follow Christ.

SUNDAY EVENING—AN IMPRESSION

" The great church is full, and the deacons are
quietly seeking room for late-comers by asking
some to sit a little closer.   There are quiet, friendly
greetings and smiles from one to another, for this
is the Father's House, and not an awesome temple.
Yet there is no chatter, for some are praying and
some still read their Bibles or hymn-books as our
fathers did, in restful meditation.   Then the blind
organist makes his way to the organ console, and
by and by very quiet music is heard.   Immediately
a hush spreads over the great congregation.   'Tis
Mr. Turner.   Dr. Morrison had a wonderful colleague, whose religious sympathy helped to make
the organ a real instrument of devotion.   The
Doctor walks slowly up the pulpit steps with an air
of deep preoccupation.   He wears neither bands
nor hood, only a gown, which will be discarded as
the service proceeds.   His hair is jet black . . . and
a very firmly set mouth, curiously reminiscent of
Dr. Whyte's, gives him a look of seriousness and
self-discipline.

" No formal phrases or Scripture quotations give
solemnity to the prayer, but a simple, natural
expression of sincere desire, couched in the natural
language of to-day.   And so it will be in the prayers
that follow.   There is a note of sympathy and
understanding which only one who has come to

know the struggles and sorrows of his people
can use. Rest and comfort, rather than striving
and high endeavour, seem to be the prevailing
note.

" Throughout the singing the preacher remains
seated, conserving his strength, and joining in the
praise, yet with an appearance of isolation, as
though his mind was too charged with what he
must say to the people. When the sermon begins,
it has a text, easily remembered, and perhaps, also
a subject with the music of poetry in its wording.
No manuscript is used. There does not even seem
to be a note to help the preacher. But each phrase
is perfectly formed. The English is musical and
crisp, almost entirely simple Saxon. Now and again
when he has made his point, and before he enters
on another phrase, a curious, unconscious ' Yes '
escapes his lips, only audible to those about him.
He never raises his voice in passionate declamation ;
never waves his hands except for a little semi-
circular movement like a man following the rhythm
of his own words. As he moves along with his
argument, the interest grows more and more tense
until, at last, at the end of twenty minutes, the
sermon is complete, and the impression made.

" Throughout the whole service the spirit of
devotion has been maintained. The anthem and the
hymns and Psalm have been sung to music that all
know, and the organ and choir lead, and do not
drown. Then, as the congregation quietly dis-
perses, the prevailing feeling remains that here we
have been worshipping, and have been brought
before God."

THE ROUND TABLE

No experiment of the latter years of Wellington was more rich in spiritual results among his young people than the Round Table, and we give here an account of it from some of their own pens.

The Round Table started in 1921 as an experiment and unlike many experiments in churches proved an immediate and tremendous success. The reasons for this are to be found in the circumstances of the time. The War was not long past, and the young men and women of Wellington, and especially those who had been on active service, made a determined effort to grapple with the problems which it had raised in their own minds. Unable to find a solution themselves, they thought if they could get Dr. Morrison-of-the-study, rather than Dr. Morrision-of-the-pulpit things would straighten out better. In the early winter of 1920 a deputation of four, appointed by the Literary and Debating Society, waited on Dr. Morrison and explained very frankly the feelings of the young people of the church. The doctor listened patiently and

sympathetically, and at once agreed to consider very carefully the suggestions put
before him. The immediate result was a
letter from him, putting before the young
people his idea of a Round Table, and its
constitution and aims, and in his characteristic way asking for their approval !

On the syllabus, which Dr. Morrison drew
up himself, this was how the gathering was
described. " The Round Table. Meetings
for mutual help through the frank discussion
of the big things. Confined to the young
men and women of the congregation." Its
motto followed—" Prove all things ;   hold
fast that which is good."

For the discussions of each session there
was a general title. One year, " The Outlook
of our Lord." Another year, " Problems of
Youth," or " Questionings of Youth." For
each meeting there was one subject for discussion. These subjects were graded with a
consummate art that I dare say few of us
were aware of at the time. For, while all
the discussions were on subjects that we
knew to be both living and pressing, the
session usually opened with one which was
fairly simple and practical, of a type on

which people were ready and anxious to speak. As the session went on, however, the subjects on the syllabus, though still as practical as ever, became such that they called for a good deal of thought on the part of the speakers, and finally we were asked to consider some of the great problems that have never yet been solved. Thus, on the first night, we would be invited to discuss the problem of the right use of Sunday. Next time, the problem of Friendship, in any of its branches, was open for discussion ; or the debate might be on such a subject as this, " What would be the outlook of our Lord on amusements ? " Another time, " How has the Church helped me ?—or failed to help me ? "

Then the discussion began to go a little deeper, thus, " What is there in Christ that appeals to me ? " ; and as the session wore on, such subjects as these would appear : " Is there a life after death ? " " Is prayer reasonable ? " and then, finally, " What is the attraction of the Cross ? "

To open the discussion two people were appointed beforehand for each night, the first speaker being allowed about ten minutes,

and the second five, in order to introduce the
subject.   The meeting was then thrown open
for general discussion.   The meetings were
held in the library of the church, and this
room was packed to the utmost every night.
In these circumstances it was not surprising
that a considerable number of those who
filled the room every Sunday evening could
never find confidence to take part in the discussions.   The idea of addressing some one
hundred and twenty of their fellows appalled
them, and they remained silent participants
in, though keen listeners to, all that was said
and rarely missing a single meeting.

It was a curious thing, however, that when
one of us, taking our courage in both hands,
had attempted a " maiden speech "—a little
halting sometimes and generally ending up
with the words—" Er, I think that's all I've
got to say "—but still frank and meaning
what they said, they generally spoke again
either the next Sunday or the one after,
and the explanation was this.   We had gone
home feeling that we had made a miserable
mess of it and that in our nervousness we
had forgotten half of our best points ; and
then, on the Monday evening, there would

be a post card waiting for us with something like this on it : " Thank you. That was admirable—just and true and well put. Do stand in often.—' G. H. M.' "

Then our confidence came back to us at once. We knew that at least one person had seen what we were driving at and had appreciated that we had tried to be candid. The consequence was that towards the end of the session when the subjects were growing harder there was still a discussion and generally a good one too. If he had not told us that he appreciated our help and, moreover, was counting on it, I don't know that many of us would have dared to raise our voices when we were invited to say what we thought about some of the central things.

As for the discussions themselves, Dr. Morrison allowed us a wide liberty in all we said, always with this condition, that what we said must be sincere. There was to be no saying of a thing merely because we thought it was the correct thing to say. He did not in the least mind unorthodox opinions, but what he did mind was anything in the nature of a flippant or trivial remark (quite distinct from a humorous one) in the middle of a serious debate. He never showed his disapproval in any way beyond the gentlest hint, yet the offenders always felt it, and generally there were no more foolish remarks that session.

The Round Table had two unwritten rules. The first of these was, that everything said there was to be regarded as said *in camera* ; and the second, that no reference to Wellington Church or to its minister was permitted. The rule regarding the secrecy of the discussions was, of course, not easy to enforce, and occasionally one heard of enthusiastic people going home and describing the whole proceedings to the rest of the household, omitting nothing, either of the personalities or of what they said. For the most part, however, it was loyally observed, and many a parent had to confess that they " could get nothing out of " their son or daughter about what had occurred. Quite often speakers came near to breaking the second rule, usually by some thinly camouflaged compliment to either church or minister. But while the rest of us generally seized the occasion to give a little applause, the chairman used to interpose at once with a firm but genial cry of, " Order, order ! "

The atmosphere at the debates was always very informal and while new speakers used often to begin with the conventional words, " Mr. Chairman, Ladies and Gentlemen," they generally dropped that before long and used the more intimate " Dr. Morrison and friends."

As regards the scope of the discussion, Dr. Morrison not only allowed, but encouraged the greatest freedom of speech, provided always, as I have said, that it was sincere. For a few sessions he used to put in the syllabus some suggested sub-headings for each subject, but latterly these were withdrawn and speakers had to think for themselves what things would be relevant to the subject for the evening. At many a meeting he heard strange theories advanced and indeed he once said, with a smile, " I hear things stated with the greatest confidence that in all my ministry I have never been quite sure of." At the same time, what impressed most of us when we had propounded what we thought was a very advanced view of some subject, was that

we found that he had been there before us,
and he would tell us with the greatest im-
partiality the arguments for and against
it, and then the conclusion he had come
to about it—whether it was of God or
not.

The common feature that one noticed in
everyone's contribution to the discussion was
the desire to know what would be our Lord's
view on the subject ; and that desire was
simply the result of Dr. Morrison's influence.
For in all his preaching his one aim had
been to show us the attractiveness of Christ,
and more than that, he had convinced us
that all that we valued as life, as opposed to
mere existence, was, as it were, concentrated
in Him. The consequence was that we had
all come to think it in the highest degree
reasonable, to try to put ourselves in our
Lord's place and see through His eyes. I
believe there were none of us but were quite
certain that we had the unseen Guest amongst
us at these meetings. Yet they were not in
the least emotional gatherings. Everyone
was in a reasonable frame of mind and there
were often humorous interludes. Somehow,
all the same, we knew that we had a Visitor

and we all tried to keep the conversation on His level.

At every debate, however, what we valued most was the chairman's summing up at the end. We had taken him into our confidence and he always repaid that by taking us into his. He never talked down to us in the least. Instead he told us fearlessly what his own views were, or what he thought was the solution of some problem, even if these were by no means orthodox. His first loyalty was to Christ and then to the Church only as it was also loyal to the same Lord. The consequence was that there was a wonderful freedom and freshness about all he said. There was never the feeling that he was telling us to believe something he himself did not, simply because we ought to believe it.

He used to say that he had no sympathy with asceticism ; that though many of God's gifts could be dangerous and were capable of abuse, still they were sent to lend colour to our life and were given us richly to enjoy, and he thought that if we rejected them instead of accepting them gladly we were showing Him not respect but ingratitude.

G

Many of us who had been troubled about these things loved him for that.

At the same time, no one was more keenly aware than he was of the power and fascination of evil. Yet he never lectured us about it. Rather, he tried to show us the futility of expecting to get abundant life from it; that the universe was governed by laws that made that impossible. He once said, " Never forget, if you are tempted to explore it, that the sensual infinite doesn't exist; it's a delusion." When he convinced us of that, he brought reason to the help of conscience and made us twice as strong as we were before.

In all that he said, however, he used to try, as he had taught us to try, to see what would be our Lord's view. But then the difference between him and us was that he had been dwelling constantly in his Master's company, and so he would speak to us about Him quite naturally, quoting Him as one might quote a friend. And in our hearts we used to feel that he had got at the core of the matter and that he had guided us rightly.

Always in his summing up he could lift the discussion to the highest level. Partly this

was because he grasped at once the funda-
mental difficulty or problem, and dealt with
it by what both he and we knew was the
only adequate method, and partly because
he had a genius for clothing all he said in
simple but shining words. Thus one night
there had been a discussion on the Church,
in the course of which all its faults and fail-
ings, as well as its virtues, had been thoroughly
aired. Various cures for its shortcomings had
been suggested, and then Dr. Morrison spoke.
He never made notes during the discussion,
yet he touched on all the points that had been
raised, going over them in order, and then, as
usual, he went straight to the root of it all.
For he said something like this :

" Various cures have been suggested for a
state of things in the Church that we all feel
is very far from what He would have. But
my feeling is that none of these goes deep
enough. For I don't think that things will
ever be right until, like a tide, God's Holy
Spirit sweeps across the Church, and then all
these difficulties will vanish away."

There was one of Dr. Morrison's characteristics that I used to notice particularly at
the Round Table meetings, though it was

evident at all the things he took part in. I
think I might describe it best by saying that
he had a great sense of an occasion. The
effect on those in the room was that they had
a sudden feeling in their minds, " Well, Dr.
Morrison's here. So things will really happen
at this meeting." The explanation, I think,
was this : Dr. Morrison, at every gathering
he attended, came with the determination to
give it of his very best.

I mentioned his summing up in a previous
paragraph. If you wish the Round Table to
illustrate some trait of the Doctor's, why not
take his wonderful power of extempore speech ?
In this, he was the Mozart of Theology.
How often, faced with the most diverse
pronouncements from the two extremes of
opinion, has he taken them *all* and worked
them into one splendid whole, omitting
nothing of importance, emphasising what was
particularly striking, and producing a harmony from the most conflicting themes with
apparently effortless skill. You ask me why
I thought people came to the Round Table ?
Well, quite a few came to hear what Dr.
Morrison would say.

It is an interesting question why the rest

came. Only a very small proportion came with the intention of giving vocal vent to their opinions, and it is unlikely that the dumb remainder came merely to give moral support to the speakers, since, as anyone who spoke can testify, the result was quite the reverse. I think the conditions under which the discussion was conducted were peculiarly attractive ; I mean, that the condition as to secrecy, although it is hardly possible that it was rigidly adhered to, gave promise of a revelation of engagingly unorthodox opinions, if you will excuse the popular inaccuracy of the adjective, and certainly it is improbable that many of the things said inside that room were ever heard in any other part of the same building. There was an *intimate* atmosphere about the thing, if you understand. Dr. Morrison was not enthroned on a pulpit high above the heads of anyone else, a position which, I learned, he found rather trying sometimes ; he occupied an ordinary chair within a few feet of the front bench. He was " one of us " in a manner which his very eminence rendered impossible anywhere else, and I know when I was speaking, I felt as if there were just the

two of us in his own library—once the awful
first word was out. He was never either
fatherly or domineering—I don't know which
is the more unbearable—he was always just a
young man who happened to have lived a good
deal longer than most of us, and whom we
respected as our indisputable leader.

You see, I have tried to say something
about the Round Table, and here I am back
at Dr. Morrison again. I cannot think of
the words without at once having my mind
flooded with memories of that great figure.

For Dr. Morrison himself, even though the
Round Table came at the end of a day in
which he had been spending himself lavishly
in the service of his Master, it did not seem
to be a strain. He was at home among his
young people, and at home in the friendly
library (for which he had a peculiar fondness)
with its bright lights and cheerful fire. The
discussions kept him in touch with the difficulties and doubts of youth and not infre-
quently, as he himself avowed, supplied him
with matter for the pulpit.

I have often seen him come in tired; I
have never seen him come in half asleep.
It did not matter whether his part at a meet-

ing was to be a large one or only a small one,
for him, all that seemed to count was that here
was a company of people ready to be shown
divine things and that therefore here there
was given him a priceless opportunity to do
something for the Master he loved. But not
only did he come determined to give of his best,
he also came with almost boundless expecta-
tions. He never confessed it in so many
words, but the feeling of it was infectious
and so we, too, came to expect great things
at these meetings. Looking back on them
after an interval of nearly two years, when
any ephemeral influence must have passed
away, I can say in all calmness that we
got them. Through the Round Table, Dr.
Morrison, it has often seemed to me, took the
promise, " Seek and ye shall find," and
verified it before our eyes.

THE PRAYER MEETING

From the middle of October to the end of
March, Dr. Morrison looked forward to meeting more closely some of his people on
Wednesday evenings in the library of the
church. He seemed to have an affection for
the library room, which held well over one

hundred people, preferring it to the larger hall, thus making the meeting a homely gathering of those he called with a touch of humour "The elect and the select." Immediately after eight o'clock he entered the room, preceded by Mr. Turner, and the buzz of friendly talk ceased, and a quiet hush fell upon all. There was always a big, bright fire burning in the fire-place at the end of the hall, at the side of which was a large table where Dr. Morrison sat.

With a few simple opening words of prayer he brought the hearts and minds of the little audience into tune with the Infinite, and so the meeting began. After the singing of a hymn and the reading of the lesson, which was undertaken by a member present—he would call on one or two of the people present to engage in prayer. Sometimes this would be arranged beforehand, but very often it was not. It was not only the men who took part in this way, as Wellington was very rich in those who had the true gift of prayer, and many were the beautiful petitions I have heard offered by the Church Sister or some lady greatly interested in Congregational or Mission work. The last person to pray finished with the Lord's Prayer, in which all joined.

For several years back, Dr. Morrison allotted " A Missionary Five Minutes," which proved of great interest to all, and helped to keep burning brightly the traditional missionary interest of Wellington Church. Extracts were generally read from the letter of a church member in the Mission field, or from a doctor, nurse or teacher engaged in some branch of missionery work in distant lands, telling of his or her work and problems. When a real live missionary was present, or any minister representing a church in other lands, the five minutes was extended to ten.

Each Wednesday evening, Dr. Morrison liked to refer to members of the congregation who were sick, in bereavement, or any kind of trouble, and gave the latest bulletin or information. He always asked in his kindly way that anyone who lived near the home or hospital would call to inquire or leave flowers. In this way mutual interest and sympathy were kept alive, and very many responded to this request.

The prayer meeting was not advertised except by pulpit intimation, but visitors

from far-off lands and other churches frequently found their way into the circle, and
many a minister or student would come to
get inspiration to help him in his present
task or future life-work. A party of Colonial
students once considered it worth while
coming through from Edinburgh to visit a
prayer meeting at Wellington.

Always alive to the importance of making
the members of the Mission Church feel that
they were in reality members of Wellington,
and that their interests were mutual, Dr.
Morrison, several times each season, had a
baptismal service at the close of the prayer
meeting, and sometimes six or even more
mission mothers (and husbands if possible)
would be present, and after the baptisms
were over each baby was presented with a
bunch of flowers by a little girl specially asked
for this purpose. At the close of the meeting
all present had an opportunity of admiring
the babies, and speaking to the proud parents.
This was always a particularly sweet and
solemn little service, and helped to link in
friendship and interest the Mission and
Church members.

Dr. Morrison always believed in teaching

from the Scriptures. He was a teacher born
and bred. One of his courses was on " Personal Interviews of Jesus " and the year of
his passing—1928—was the Bunyan tercen-
tenary, and he had prepared to give addresses
on scenes in " The Pilgrim's Progress." He
also believed in intensive devotional preparation for the quarterly communion, and
in addition to the pre-communion service,
there was always a short Saturday night
prayer meeting on the eve of the Sacrament.
The prayers on that occasion were specially
heart-searching. He knew the value of a
good question, and one memorable short
address was on " What think ye, that He
will not come to the Feast ? " and gracious
assurance was given to longing souls.

After the benediction the Doctor always
stood at the door and shook hands with everyone as they passed out. This habit he
learned when, during his fourth year at
Glasgow College, he acted as missionary to
the Rev. George Clazy, in Oakshaw Free
Church, Paisley. All through his ministry
he kept up this habit, and to many the kindly
smile or handshake, or a few words of
sympathetic inquiry, were just the perfect

finish to that mid-week hour of quiet communion and spiritual uplift.

Even after he had said " Good night " to
the last person and seen any who remained
behind for special help or talk, his labours
for the night were not ended. He went to
the vestry, where he discussed special cases
and went over the week's work with the
Church Sister. Then he changed into an old
jacket, which was kept in the vestry for him,
and commenced dictating to his secretary,
who was always in attendance after the prayer
meeting. They worked steadily until ten-
thirty, and often much later. In fact, it was
frequently long after eleven when he returned
home.

Miss Janey Lambie, who for many years
acted as hon. secretary to Dr. Morrison with
a loyalty, efficiency, and devotion that no
pen could ever do justice to, did not long
survive the minister to whom she gave so
unstintingly of her time and talents. Within
three months of his going, she too left us,
after a very brief illness. For many years
she had held a responsible and honourable
post in one of the large Assurance offices in
Glasgow, and consequently had little time to

give to church work, but as the Session Clerk of Wellington, has truly written, " Along the line she could best serve, in her spare time giving valuable help to Dr. Morrison in secretarial work, she delighted to serve, a service he deeply appreciated, and in his semi-jubilee address, warmly acknowledged." By her quiet and unassuming ways, and her sweetness of disposition, she endeared herself to many in the church, and to Dr. Morrison and myself and family she was a loved and trusted friend.

Although the prayer meeting ended at the beginning of March, and there was a break until after Easter, Dr. Morrison usually conducted a short series of Wednesday evening services, beginning in the end of April, and continuing to the end of May. These meetings, he said, were primarily for those who were unable to face the dark, cold nights in winter, but frequently so many attended that they had to be held in the large hall. Then came the June Monday lectures, to which special reference is made elsewhere, and as there was always a week of special meetings at the beginning of October, there were really only about four months in the year without a mid-week service.

All this meant a tremendous amount of preparation, and, in addition, from October until Christmas, he held his Bible Class after the evening service. At this class, the body of the church was well filled, and as a rule he spoke without notes for forty minutes.

I am adding a list of some of the subjects he took for his Bible Class, between the years 1921 to 1928 :

Christ and other masters.
Problems of our faith.
The inward life of literature.
Heresies of to-day.
Religion in modern literature.
Christ in Shakespeare, etc. etc.

From the middle of January until the middle of March the " Round Table " met after evening service.

AMONG HIS MISSION PEOPLE

The Missions were not exempt from the scope of his great activities, and the enthusiasm which he displayed there, made one almost believe that it was his sole interest in life. Even when Moderator of the Church, he was not too busy to go down to the Missions and give a warm handshake to

everyone present. He understood their difficulties and trials, as if he lived with them
every day, and for this the people loved and
adored him.

A minister on being taken round the
various meetings in the Mission district one
Sunday night, after preaching forenoon and
afternoon in the church, remarked, "It is
magnificent, but Wellington is not a congregation, it is a diocese."

Any description of Dr. Morrison would be
incomplete that contained no reference to
the part he took in the home mission work of
the church. When he came to Glasgow it
was to a congregation with whom direct home
mission effort in their own city was almost
an article of faith. They had been brought
up to look upon it as part of their religious
life, and in two separate centres, both
situated in the populous dockland district of
the north bank of the river, a very considerable number of Wellington members and
adherents were engaged every week as
teachers, monitors, visitors, bankers, officers
of Boys' Brigade and Girls' Guildry Companies, or, at the least, as occasional speakers
at Sunday and weekday meetings for old

and young.   An unordained missionary super-
intended the Mission Church in Piccadilly
Street, with its 300 members attached to
Wellington congregation, and two Church
Sisters by daily visitation kept the congregational committees in touch with the homes
and lives of the people. Those who have
already gained some insight into Dr. Morrison's
temperament and outlook will recognise that
this side of his congregational work could not
fail to appeal strongly to him.   The actuality
itself was impressive. When he preached
from his own pulpit, probably 300 of his
regular hearers were busy men and women
voluntarily engaged in helping their less
fortunate citizens, and that by their own
personal endeavour. They were his fellow-
workers, and to have them associated with
him was an encouragement and support in
the arduous and ceaseless duties of his
ministry. Then too, though a student, he
was no recluse. He loved the people and
enjoyed fellowship with them.   Consequently
into this part of his congregation's work he
entered heartily at all times, not only with a
sympathetic interest but, as he often assured
the workers, with a lively sense of the great-

ness of their task and its importance to the city and to the church.

It may well be wondered how, with the close attention he gave to his pulpit ministry in the church and the enormous demands that pastoral visitation made on his time, he could find opportunity to be present at these mission halls, both situated about two miles from his church and manse.   But if he could not find the opportunity he created it, and in the arrangement of his time he was a master of method.   On the four Communion Sundays a stranger occupied the Wellington pulpit in the evening, and these evenings he set aside for visiting the Mission Sunday Schools, greeting the teachers and occasionally saying a few words to the children.

In such movements as the Boys' Brigade and the Girls' Guildry, Dr. Morrison's interest was deep and personal.   The Boys' Brigade was born in the congregation in which he was brought up, and the west of Glasgow where he laboured had also been the nursery of the Guildry.   For the young men and women who carried on this work, and in those under their charge in the Missions, he had a very special interest, and to be present at their

H

annual inspections gave him genuine and manifest pleasure. It was his great delight and usual practice to have these Companies parading at church once every year, and on such occasions their minister's addresses, like those he gave to the young people of the congregation, were memorable both for their subject and for the lightness of touch with which it was presented to the mind of youth.

The [communion services in the Piccadilly Mission Church, which ranked as occasions of great importance and significance to Dr. Morrison, were always attended by a large proportion of its members, and were conducted by himself with the assistance of the Wellington Session. A baptismal service, at which three, four or even half a dozen infants were presented, very often preceded the communion. Dr. Morrison's addresses on these occasions were generally characterised by a special warmth of feeling as he welcomed the members to the Lord's Table. He had a deep and tender sympathy for these men and women, both young and old, most of them hedged about in a special degree by daily uncertainties, yet putting up a gallant fight and bearing a cheerful front amid conditions that depressed and might easily have depraved. Nowhere was he listened to with closer attention ; nowhere was he himself held in higher honour as the bearer of that message. For wherever he might appear among the mission folk, whether as preacher or as the genial chairman at a Mothers' Meeting tea, or as visitor at their summer excursions on the Clyde, where he and Mrs. Morrison were confidently expected to appear at some time of the day, he was always and evidently their friend, rejoicing to be among them, one in whom they could trust.

CHAPTER VI

WITH HIS FAMILY AND YOUNG FRIENDS

" THE DOCTOR " was surely characterised by nothing more than by his generous and deep affection for all young people. His love for them was the instinctive gesture of the big and strong towards the lesser and weaker. It was a very wise love ; he never preached at them (or at anybody, for that matter) but was wont in his utterances to draw pictures for them that, in conception and in sheer simplicity of expression alike, revealed him as the poet he was. (It may be that the unselfish are always poets.) For the rest, he mingled with his young people, lived before them and was himself, and taking these one with the other, they found in him a goodness and sufficiency and charm ; and, above all, a big and downright manhood that attracted and satisfied and, not a little, inspired them.

For their part, being young, the response was free and generous, and to him, very precious; for, being spontaneous, it did not calculate, and, being young, it was warm; and being both, it refreshed him and gave him the assurance that could not but be pleasing, that in himself youth was vigorous and veritably identified with all Youth.

It cannot be hard for those who knew him to understand how strong and mutually binding were the ties that existed between the Doctor and the young folk of his congregation; but it must pass the comprehension of any less a master in the use of time than he was, to understand how he contrived to devote to them collectively and individually so many precious hours. Indeed, it would be deeply interesting and illuminating to know just precisely how much of his time he did spend in this way. How he spent it those who shared it with him know and will never forget; and if to be with him in a company was a happy experience, a private interview with him naturally enough was not only happy, but memorable. There must be very few to whom, at one time or another, he did not give for a little space his undivided attention. It was a wonderful experience and one left him feeling strangely light of foot, to find perhaps that our friendly, comfortable, wordly old Glasgow had become mysteriously changed of face, a new city clothed in undreamed-of poetry, and full of heart-quickening spells. "The singing of birds" that the Doctor so often spoke about, became in one's heart a very definite reality.

Loved as the Doctor was by all young people and children, it is not surprising that, to his own family, he was ever the adored and adoring father.

With his wonderfully boyish spirit, his vast capacity for fun and nonsense, and his keen sense of humour and mischief, he proved at all times a delightful companion, and was ever the interested helper in all games and adventures. He had a marvellously correct eye for perspective and all kinds of drawing and printing, and I have inserted in this chapter a specimen of his pen sketches representing a duel. To children his post cards and letters were always charming, and lit by a freshness and understanding that made them treasured possessions.

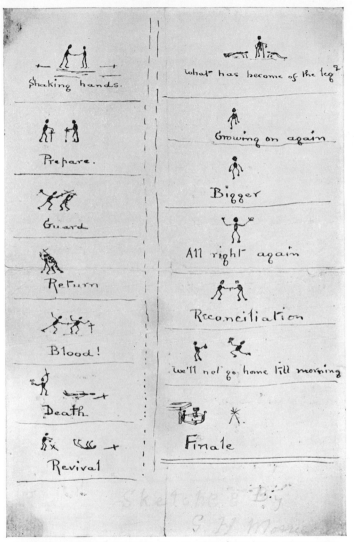

Shaking hands.

Prepare.

Guard

Return

Blood!

Death

Revival

What has become of the leg?

Growing on again

Bigger

All right again

Reconciliation

we'll not go home till morning

Finale

STORY OF A DUEL DRAWN BY DR. MORRISON ON A POST CARD

In a life so fully occupied, it was inevitable that he could not see so much of his family as he would have liked, and many were the murmurs from the children about the hard fate of having a busy minister for a father. But in holiday time he tried to make up for this deficiency by devoting a great deal of time to them.

The forenoon hours, as I have already said, were always sacred to study, but the hour between breakfast and ten o'clock was considered the children's hour, and I have many memories of him wandering along country roads, through the woods, or by the seashore, hung round by an eager, adoring group of small folk who listened entranced while he spun tales for them, or guided their feet in the first steps of field botany.

An enthusiastic and successful botanist himself from his schooldays, he taught his children to keep an open eye for the treasures of nature that lay all around their feet in field and hedgerow and, to the very end, his own keen eye never missed the tiniest plant by the wayside or the first coltsfoot or celandine of spring.

A daughter writes :

" Little pictures of him keep coming to my mind. The Christmases of long ago ! The dining-room table on Christmas morning covered with a large white sheet under which lay all our presents, and as a sign that none of us must touch or peep underneath, he had painted a large skull and cross bones on paper and pinned it on to the sheet. Even after all these years I can still see the skull grinning at us, and I don't think one of us ever attempted a stolen look. Another picture is of walking with him in lovely woods on a summer day in the holidays, and my surprise and joy when I saw lying on a mossy tree-trunk a bright silver sixpence, and my exclamation, ' Oh, daddy, look what I've found,' and then the twinkle in his eyes, the ready smile and ' Well done ! I put it there to teach you to be observant.'

" How vividly, too, can I remember, how we used to stand at the nursery window to wave to him day by day as he went down the Gardens, and always at the same spot he would turn and look up with a smile, and then make a great pretence of having bumped into the lamp post. How we loved that little bit of play-acting and watched for it daily. There are so many things I could write of. What a wonderful sense of peace and security seemed to be all around when he was there. He never once in all the years preached *at* us. His religion and his simple faith were with him and around him all the time. It seems to me, looking back now, that his whole life was one long sermon of great humility and loving thoughtfulness, and if in my childish ignorance my eyes were blind to the greatness of him, they have been opened now to realise the unfailing father-love that was ever underneath all he said and did for us."

After the children grew bigger, we all possessed cycles and used to go out, a family party of six, for long runs and picnics. For a number of years the summer holidays were spent in the Kyles of Bute or at Arran, where boating, bathing and fishing were the daily occupations, and no one entered more fully into the fun than the Doctor. Picnics he adored, but a picnic was not a real picnic to him unless there was a good fire. Spirit lamps and thermos flasks he scorned, and to him was always allotted the task of lighting the real wood fire.

As years went on, and the taste of the family turned to golf and tennis, we went inland, and spent several seasons at Edzell in Forfarshire, but once we had journeyed north of the Grampians, and been caught by the glamour of lovely Speyside and the Cairngorms, our allegiance to the North never wavered, and summer after summer found us back, latterly at Nethybridge, which we loved best of all.

It was while at Newtonmore that the shadows of war first fell on us, and the next four years with their devastating sorrows and anxieties broke up all happy united holidays. George, the eldest son, was a prisoner in Germany for three years, Kathleen, the eldest girl, off to war service in London, Sandy into training the moment he was of age to join up, and Alison off to boarding school and, from there, to work with the Imperial War Graves Commission at St. Omer, so that never again after 1914 were we all together a united family.

The Doctor's keen sense of humour and capacity for enjoying and entering into all fun drew to him hosts of young people during the holidays, who were keen to have him with them on all occasions, and the following letters and verses show different moods in dealing with them.

One day whilst staying at Nethybridge, a daughter of the minister undertook to post the Doctor's letters. Hurriedly he calculated the cost and said, " You may keep the change, which will be 3d., and buy sweets with it." He had, however, miscalculated, and next time they met she said she had not the courage to ask for a halfpenny worth of sweets, which was all the change left after paying for the stamps. The next day a box of chocolates was left at the Manse, with the accompanying lines :

Dear K., you must have thought it strange
To get one halfpenny of change,
But I was never good at sums,
Nor will be till the Kingdom comes.
I pictured you, the letters sent,
Proceeding home in sweet content,
With toffee balls or chocolate beans
Bought in that precious store of Deans.
Alas ! thanks to my gross mistake
The total balance was—one *make*
On which would gently fall (I fear)
The secret tribute of a tear.
The loss was yours ; the error mine
(At figures never did I shine).
Forgive.   Accept.   Do not condemn
That sorry bungler G. H. M.

LINES

Written by the late Dr. Morrison of Wellington U.F. Church, Glasgow, in a girl's album, dated 1905.

You ask me, lady, in this quiet time,
  To pen a poem, and to spoil a page ;
But I have lost the gentle art of rhyme
  For quite an age.

Yet though my verses had a youthful close,
  My passion for rich melody remains ;
And perhaps there is some music in my prose,
  Thanks to these pains.

For I believe that all our songs which died,
  And all our lost and ineffectual lays,
Come back to us, transfigured, glorified,
  In after days.

Until I learn this lesson from the strife—
  That by the lights which sink, the dreams which
    fail—
Somehow we are made ready for the life
  Beyond the veil.

Letter to a daughter after spending a day
in London with her, during which she took
him into a shop to buy him a tie and came
out without making a purchase :

MY DARLING LOVE,

      Now that the day is done,
I sit and think how all the hours have run,
Since the glad instant when you rang the bell
To the accursèd moment of farewell.
It was a ripping day—one of the best.
And (coz I love you) I was quite at rest
(Save when I shrank to half my normal size,
In the blank horror of refusing ties).
Now lest you're anxious in your loving way
That I was over-wearied with the day,

Learn that I caught a train to Finchley Road,
Saw the Macfarlanes in their sweet abode ;
Came home and had a bath and changed my clothes,
And entered on a period of repose.
First a delightful meal, of tea and fowl,
All by my lonesome—not another sowl—
Then to my chair here, by the parlour fire,
With pipe and *Punch* (what more could man desire ?)
Till now, remembering the hours that flew,
I gaze into the smoke and dream of you.
Good was the shining of the morning rays,
Good was the salmon and the mayonnaise,
Good was the taxi, where we were all alone,
Good was the scenery of Rodney Stone,
Good were the streets, with all their human tide,
BUT, best of all to have you by my side.
So happy, grateful, privileged and blest,
I lay my pen aside, and go to rest,
Feeling that life has something rich and true,
So long as you have me and I have you.
God bless you !   When I survey this curious scene,
And think of what a failure I have been,
One thing comes whisp'ring that I've been forgiven,
One thing comes holding out some hope of heav'n ;
ONE THING stands out, glorious amid the bad—
That *I* was pre-ordained to be your DAD.

Among the young people of the congregation, especially those whom he had baptised
and watched lovingly as they grew through
childhood to youth, he was a much loved and
trusted friend, and it was one of the big joys
in his ministry to feel that they would turn

to him in their difficulties, as well as asking him to share in their pleasures and interests. He was adopted uncle to quite a number, and his influence on many young minds and characters is indelibly graven.

One of his typical letters to an adopted niece:

" MY DEAREST NIECE,

" I cannot tell you how glad I was to get your letter, and especially to learn from it that the world was looking different to you now from what it did a while ago. We have all got to battle our way along through a good deal of unhappiness, but the sun is sure to shine if we keep loyally to what is best. I often think of you and breathe a little prayer for you, and you don't know what a joy it is to me to see you growing up into winsome and noble womanhood. I have always been proud of you and loved to have your friendship, and you must give it to me right on to the end. So long as you love and trust me and turn to me should you need a friend (like a bird to its nest) I shall be proud and happy. The one thing I could not bear would be that you should put me outside your life. Take good care of yourself, and keep your face towards the sunrise, and for Heaven's sake don't get critical of everything as so many girls to-day seem to be. In a mood like that one always misses the best.

" My love to you now and always,

" Your affectionate Uncle,

" GEORGE H. MORRISON."

Letter to a girl who had faced a difficult sorrow :

" DEAR ———,

" My wife often tells me I am not canny, and it must be so. Surely it was of God that on Sunday— why I know not—my thoughts went out powerfully, affectionately and prayerfully to you, and now this morning your note comes. My poor girl. I am truly sorry for you at this time, but God has been leading you so surely and steadily to the light and to service that all is going to be well. Open your heart wide and constantly to Him. Let Him in, in all the power and joy of the Divine Life and ' weeping may endure for a night, but joy cometh in the morning.'

" Write and tell me all about your new life. You are dear to me, and your spiritual life is precious to me, and remember that when we meet THE FIRST THING I am going to see is that new light upon your face.

" Affectionately yours,
" G. H. MORRISON."

To a young teacher on holiday :

" 29, Lilybank Gardens,
" Spring, 1918.

" MY DEAR ———,

" It was good to have the mists parting and through the mists to have a glimpse of you. In other words, it was good to hear from you, and especially so when all the news is good. How often have I thought of you both ; and I have sometimes felt that in quiet moments of retreat you were not forgetting me.

"How good the world is just now! Even Glasgow is making a gallant effort to be beautiful; and if Glasgow, how much more Skye? But the beauty of Skye, like that of Heaven, is effortless. Love to Effie. It is fine to hear that she is so much stronger and able to face work again.

"We are all well, and not idle; but we manage to possess our souls. How overpowering at times is the Divine Presence. One feels it as the tremendous reality.

"I get glimpses of Mary, who is behaving in spite of your absence. When are you coming back? We miss you.

"Ever dear,
"Affectionately,
"G. H. MORRISON."

Feeling sure that it would interest readers to know something of the relationship which existed between the minister and the young men in the congregation, I asked one whom Dr. Morrison had known from his birth to write me an impression, which he has done on the understanding that he shall remain anonymous.

DR. MORRISON

(AS HE APPEARED TO YOUNG PEOPLE)

The writer of this appreciation would say at the outset that he can, of course, only speak for himself and give his own impressions, with perhaps those of a few others who have told him something of what they owed to their minister. In a sense this is a tribute to the particular way in which Dr. Morrison commended himself to young people. For the reader will understand that if he had been, let us say, only a genial friend and an interesting preacher, then any young person who knew him could without a thought have given their opinion of him. But as he stood for something very intimate to us and made his strongest appeal to the deeper side of our nature, much cannot be said about him except as to some trusted friend.

Probably the greatest cause at the back of our affection for him was this, that none of us ever felt we were condemned in his eyes or even disapproved of because he did not understand us or our difficulties. We might tell him of temptations that had never troubled him, yet we knew at once from what he said (or didn't say) that he saw how powerful they were for us. Moreover, instead of falling in his estimation because we were tempted at all, we felt that we went up in his regard if we were making a good fight.

I

So many people are apt, almost unconsciously, to think that there is little difference between those who are tempted and those who yield. Just another word about this genius of his for understanding people. There is perhaps nothing more discouraging when one is talking to a friend than suddenly realising that one has passed the limits of his comprehension, or else that what one is now saying interests him so little that he is simply not troubling to follow. It was just the opposite of this that was apparent in speaking to Dr. Morrison. What was said might not attract him in itself, but because it concerned someone in whom he was interested he would talk about it with an intelligence that often made one wonder if he did not know far more about it than he would admit. It may be quite true to say that this ability to look not only on one's own things, but also on the things of others is of the essence of good breeding ; but then it needs power of mind as well as sympathy of heart. So, although Dr. Morrison in his modesty never made the least parade of his intellect, there must have been few who did not feel after talking with him that they had been in

touch with a mind of first-class quality.
This feeling was often strongest when the
conversation had been only of ordinary
things—not poetical or mystical in the least
—for he had the power, which is agreed to
be a hallmark of genius, of making simple
things great.

There was another discovery made in conversation with him that perhaps some may
question, and yet I am sure it was true. It
was this : that he was one who found friendship difficult and to whom its attainment was
always an effort. Yet it was exactly this
quality that endeared him even more to
many of us, for nearly everyone who gets a
gift values it according to what it has cost
the giver. And if this is often true when
people are giving us things, it is always true
when they are giving us themselves. We
have many friends whose company is delightful because they are by nature genial and
sincere and understanding, but we have
others, who, though they have these things
all locked up inside them, seem able to get
them out only after years of striving and,
I suppose, of prayer. But when at last they
succeed there is a peculiar quality about their

friendship that makes us instinctively put it
in a class by itself. In his later years especially one noticed Dr. Morrison's natural shyness much less, for it had been succeeded by
a wonderful geniality, yet the feeling that
he had only achieved it *per ardua* made one
value it far more than if it had been merely
the product of a sort of facile good nature.
I don't think we admired him less because
he found " small talk " difficult. After all,
so many of the people we knew could only
give the small change of conversation and,
while that made talking to them a very
effortless business, it also inevitably cheap-
ened it. On the other hand, Dr. Morrison's
mind seemed to have found its natural home
amongst the eternal things, and the consequence was that when we were reaching out
towards them and were longing to talk about
them with someone who knew and loved
them we could count on him to meet us *there*.
None knew better than he, however, that we
could not always reach these high levels.
For the meeting might be only a casual and
short one—on a tramcar or on the doorstep
of someone's house. Yet, even then, when
we had only a word or two with him, we felt

better for having seen him. What he said was always well chosen, for he had an uncanny way of remembering, at a moment's notice, all about us. He had also a peculiar way of looking directly at us when we were talking, which was at first rather disconcerting, though afterwards we grew to look for it and to love it. It was as if he were saying, " Yes, I know you have lots of things you would like to talk about but you feel this isn't the time ; but I understand and we'll have a great talk some other time." It recalled often Emerson's description of two friends talking together and suddenly being greater than they knew because Jove was nodding to Jove behind each of them.

There are two incidents that I heard of, both showing how he used to extend his friendliness and his courtesy quite outside the company of those he knew and without respect of social standing.

The scene of the first was a wedding reception and two girls at it had found that they knew no one and were sitting together and feeling a little out of things. Dr. Morrison saw them and came across and sat down beside them, and one of them said when she was recalling the incident, " And it wasn't as if he knew us in the least. We didn't belong to his church. But he saw that we knew no one and he came and sat beside us and talked—well, just of ordinary things. But all the same, I had never met anyone like that before."

The second incident happened at a tramcar stop at the end of the Jamaica Bridge in Glasgow. A young carter who came to Wellington Mission told of it. " I was driving my lorry towards the bridge when I had to pull up at a car station, for the rule is in Glasgow that vehicles must pull up when a tramcar has stopped. Dr. Morrison was the only person getting on to the car. I knew him, though he didn't know me. But he saw that a carter had had to stop for him, and when he had got on to the car he turned and lifted his hat."

There was one characteristic of Dr. Morrison that was probably most appreciated by those who had spent some years at the university or some place of study. It was simply this, that he kept to his work. Let me explain what I mean. What surprises every student, coming from school to the university, is just that he need not work unless he likes. On the contrary, he is encouraged to join every kind of society and to take part in all sorts of activities. He finds that in these things he can become a popular person, can become a great man in undergraduate circles. All that is quite good up to a point, but the temptation and the danger lie in regarding these as ends in themselves and activity in them as being the same as real work. For, meanwhile, his studies have received only spasmodic and irregular attention and never the first freshness of his mind. And then Nemesis inevitably overtakes him when examinations come, and if he faces things honestly he is driven to see that all these things on which he had dissipated his energy were utterly unproductive so far as any permanent results were concerned. He realises that the one road to real achievement is conscientious, unremitting work, with no immediate applause and popularity, and the next session he will not become a hermit, but he will keep the secondary things in their places and put the first things first.

When one remembers that he was by nature a student and a man of letters, one

of the striking things about him was his wide
knowledge of life. I mean by that, life as
it confronts ordinary people, some eager and
some weary, who can justly say that they
are in the thick of it. Anyone who says of
Dr. Morrison that " he was a student looking
on life through his study window " is just
wrong. Our minister knew life far more widely
and intimately than we did. Many a time he
would show by some passing remark that he
was quite aware of some phase or custom of
modern life that we never dreamt he knew
of. But he was possessed of what Americans
call " a loose-leaf mind "—a mind that had
never become set and incapable of taking in
new ideas—and when new things came to his
notice he would give them his unbiased
attention, and welcome them if he found
they were of good report. At the same time,
he was never one of those who stifle their
consciences on certain things for fear of being
considered out of date, or who think that
the eternal verities no longer hold good in
the twentieth century. I have a vivid recol-
lection of him looking round on us when the
harmlessness or otherwise of some modern
custom had been under debate, and saying :

" Well, now, I've tried to come to this with a perfectly open mind. But, you know, there are some things that are just for ever wrong, and I've a strong feeling that this is one of them." We would have challenged anyone who said that we were not typically modern young people. Yet generally, in our hearts, we could not but acknowledge that he was right.

In his dealings with individual people as well as in his views on society in general, Dr. Morrison's judgments always went deep. The froth blowing about on the surface troubled him very little ; his mind seemed always concerned with the currents beneath. I remember one young man telling him frankly that he didn't set up to be much of a Christian and that he did not feel greatly attracted to the church when he saw some of the things it did, and so on, and Dr. Morrison's rather surprising reply was something like this : " Your hand, So-and-so. I like an honest heart, and, mark me, I don't think you're far from the Kingdom."

Now, without pretending to know all about it, I venture to say that a minister's life is one where want of mental discipline is fatal, and it was just in that quality that Dr. Morrison was strongest. Most of us young people were working hard ourselves during the week, and we respected him because we saw that he worked himself as hard as we did, and often harder. Very often when we had finished our work and were coming home we would meet him still visiting, and we knew that there were very few evenings that he spent in his home. Like our work, too, his work was of the kind that needs faithfulness. He might easily have curtailed his study and his pastoral work to go and win applause at conferences or at Church courts. Without wishing to decry those who do so, I must say this, and I do not speak for myself alone, that we should have thought much less of him if he had. What we admired in him was his belief that the most effective service was direct service, given to those who needed him most.

There was one quality of Dr. Morrison's that greatly enriched the charm of his personality, and that was his language. All he said and all he wrote was conveyed in beautiful English, simple, vivid, and telling.

In his speech, as in his dress, he had the hatred of an exact mind for anything sloppy. Do not think from this that his language was elaborate and full of learned words. It was an example of the art that conceals art, and if one may say it in all reverence, it resembled the language of Another in this— that it made common people hear him gladly.

I have touched upon Dr. Morrison's frankness in speaking to us at the Round Table and elsewhere, but in all his directness I have never heard him use a slang word, unless, of course, in quotation. Many well-meaning people in addressing a meeting of their younger friends hope to make themselves intelligible to their hearers by using words they would never use on any other occasion. Few ideas could be more futile, and Dr. Morrison with the sensitiveness of an artist knew it. His talk could be, and was, informal, sincere and man-to-man in its character, but it was in good English, always. If he had done otherwise he would not have been true to himself, and we would have known it, and he would inevitably have lost something, not of our love, but of our respect.

One of the characteristics of our Lord

that seemed to have impressed Dr. Morrison deeply was his practice of giving of his best to an audience of one, as freely as to a multitude. In our minister that idea had become a principle. We have all known people who could be brilliant in public, or who could give a splendid address, and then in private company, somehow, they were disappointing. They were dull or querulous, and their little weaknesses stood out rather disconcertingly. Alone with a single companion, Dr. Morrison was still the man the crowds knew. He was still quick and eager on any intellectual topic or, better still, genuine, sympathetic, yet always giving that peculiar impression of latent power, when the conversation was on things more of the heart than the head.

In one of his books, G. K. Chesterton says : " There is a great man who makes every man feel small. But the real great man is the man who makes every man feel great." Dr. Morrison's greatness was of the second kind. He seemed to go on the assumption that his hearer was his equal in every way, and nearly always the effect on them was that they felt that they had to be worthy of his high opinion. After a talk with him one had a feeling of wonderful freedom of spirit. It was as though he lived himself in a large and warm world where all things were intensely alive and where nothing was too wonderful to happen. One of his sayings that greatly appealed to me was this : " The glory of life is its unexpectedness. If it weren't for that it wouldn't be worth living." That, of course, is not new—St. Paul knew that we are saved by hope—but one of the attractive things about Dr. Morrison was that in all he said and did he believed it, and by a kind of beneficent infection he made that attitude ours also.

I have purposely left to the end a word about the quality of Dr. Morrison that was, as it were, a crown to all the others. I once read these words by a writer who was trying to give his idea of a real man of God : " There are some men about whom the aroma of the unseen clings like incense ; who win men to a love of the highest through the impression they give that they have themselves found there their natural home." These words are peculiarly true of Dr. Morrison. I have never met anyone whose

mind dwelled so constantly amongst the
eternal things. With most of us it is a case
of striving towards the highest, and even of
taking the Kingdom by violence, but with
him there seemed to be no striving necessary.
He loved Christ with the love of the saint,
one might honestly say, and having found
in Him all that he wanted he seemed quite
untroubled by the attractions of lower things.
And yet the wonderful thing remains, that
with all his apparent immunity from ordinary
people's temptations there was never anyone
such a brother to those finding " the world,
the flesh and the devil " difficult things to
resist. He had a saying he was very fond of :
" How practical these mystics are ! " and I
think he had determined it should be true
in his case. For he was indeed a practical
mystic, and many of us know now that there
can be no stronger advocate of the case for
the Kingdom than that.

He seemed to find particular joy in the
Second Person of the Trinity, chiefly, I
think, through the feeling that most of us
would only reach an appreciation of the
other two through Him. I think we all
noticed the way in which he used to speak

of "our blessed Lord," apparently finding peculiar satisfaction in the adjective, and using the expression with increasing frequency. Many people could only have used that description with partial sincerity, but we knew that with him it was simple truth. Christ was the end, both of his preaching and his life, and any observant person could see that the thought of his Lord was the dominant one in his mind and the inspiration of every word he spoke.

In all his dealings with us he tried to put before us the vision of the highest, trusting that we would feel the strength of its appeal and would love it when we saw it. But there are many of us who know that we were first drawn to feel the attractiveness of Christ through seeing the reflection of it in the person of the disciple—who is not greater than his Lord.

The following article was written in 1926, and copied from one of Dr. Morrison's scrap-books.

THE PEOPLE WHO "QUEUE UP"

Seems to me there are two ways of attracting people—especially young people—to a church : one is to be unconventional, denounce something or laugh at some highly regarded convention ; the other way is to refuse to lower your standards, to preach what you really have felt and really mean. A fool with an imagination can do the first ; it takes a very big man to do the second. Dr. Morrison belongs to the second class. That type of preaching seems to be the only type after all ; the other loses its polish and glitter in the end. It is because we young people feel that Dr. Morrison is to be relied upon, because we feel that he understands us and does his best to help us, that we go to hear him.

Perhaps you have to be young to " know " " the Doctor." Young enough, that is, to enjoy standing in a long queue of a winter's night, the Avenue full of glittering pools of water, and a smirr falling past the flickering lamp and making music on your neighbour's umbrella, the wind rustling playfully through the trees across the pavement, waiting for the bell on the university to rumble out the quarter to seven. If you *are* young enough, a little sentimental, and very idealistic, you may be sure you will like Dr. Morrison.

It used to be said of Henry Drummond that young men did not pray to God or Christ, but to Drummond. It was an astonishing thing to say, but I am quite certain that there are many young fellows and girls, adherents of Wellington Church, who could understand that sentiment.

You will find the type of person I mean if you go to Wellington. There is the young clerk out from the Highlands who is lonely and misunderstood ; there is the apprentice engineer who has been having a particularly bad time of it in the " shop " ; there is the student struggling through examinations ; there is the typist who is feeling " fed up " about everything ; the shop girl who never reads anything heavier than the novels of Ethel M. Dell ; all of them outwardly cheerful but yet inwardly worried, and puzzled and uncertain just " where they stand." And all these youths will go back home from Wellington, confident that " the Doctor " was preaching a sermon which just fitted their case and theirs only.

Most of us—even those who find a pen a strange weapon—write to him at some time or other. We generally tell him things

K

which we " widna tell tae ony," and there is one foolish youth who wrote once without enclosing an address, and who discovered, to his surprise, that he had dropped some clue which had led to his discovery. The reply, written at the beginning of a rushing Moderatorial year, was quite long and kindly, and actually invited one to appeal to the manse if in need of help.

There are hundreds of us who have never met " the Doctor," and yet we owe almost everything we have and are to him. " And Jacob called the name of the place where God spake with him, Bethel." There is a mighty army of young people in Glasgow, and throughout the world, to-day, of all shades of political and social thought, who call it by another name.

THE CHILDREN'S MINISTER

A memory of the Doctor that I shall ever cherish is clearly photographed on my mind. Every morning, immediately after breakfast, he sat at the writing-table in the oriel window, answering letters, but was never too deeply immersed to look up as scampering feet and shrill voices told him that the tiny children of the garden who congregated in the morning to play, were passing the window, and would be looking for his attention. He used always to tap on the window and wave, or make funny faces at them, and if he failed to perform, the youngsters would climb up on the iron railing and shout to him. In summer time when our front door stood wide open, the least shy would run in and out, and wild shrieks of mirth would echo through the house. Then when he walked in the gardens in the summer mornings, he was always surrounded by little clinging arms. We were fortunate in having those delightful gardens in front of our house, with all the young life that congregated there.

Nowhere was he happier or more at home than amongst children and young people, and children and animals, with their unerring instinct, claimed and greeted him as their rightful possession and friend. With all reverence I say it, that he always reminded me in his dealings with children of His Master who was the friend of little children. From the babies he always held in his arms for baptism, and on whom he always looked with such a tender smile of blessing—so that sometimes they would smile back to him in confidence—to the bigger children in the congregation who clambered up on his knees asking for a story, or stood around with wide-open eyes of astonishment while he did marvellous tricks with pennies, making them disappear up his sleeve and come out behind his ear, and swallowing them and finding them in his shoes, he was far closer than their minister—he was their friend. He had the rare gift of gaining the confidence of even the shyest children and making them feel for the time being that he was one of themselves. I remember how in one manse, after he had played for a good long time at being a wild beast and had been creeping about the floor and under tables, he said to the small boys : " I am afraid I am a very silly man to go on like this," and how the oldest boy (now a successful minister) replied with delightful candour : " Yes, you are awfully silly, but you are very nice ! "

The Mission children all looked on him as their own special property, and many a time I have seen him take a fretful, wailing baby from the arms of a tired mother and after a few minutes hand it back to her in peaceful sleep. He always laughed and said he had a magic touch with crying babies, and indeed it seemed true.

I remember one baby which was a few months old when baptised and how it got hold of his bands and tugged at them the whole time of the ceremony, crowing joyfully. Nothing ever disturbed his calm serenity or put him off the duty on hand.

There was no part of his work that he loved better than his work amongst the young. His sermons to the children were not merely stories with a moral, but real little gems of literary thought into which he wove threads of topical subjects, history, science and nature, with consummate art while keeping very near to the great central truth—the love of Christ.

To those who were privileged to hear those bright addresses he revealed in striking fashion how, living always close to Nature's heart, he was skilled in finding " sermons in stones, books in the running brooks, and good in everything."

Mrs. Isabel Cameron writes :

" He preached children's sermons to which it was a sheer delight to listen, and which charmed the grown-ups quite as much as the bairns. ' Joy '

was one of them. ' Three little children dancing in
a ring. *Jesus* first, *ourselves* last and *you* in the
middle.'

" There was another one which we remember
even more vividly. By the word magic which was
peculiarly his own, he transported us all from the
grey, wind-swept town of Thurso to a certain eastern
town where, in the market-place, boys and girls
were playing. First they played ' weddings ' ; then
they played ' funerals.' In order to make their play
thoroughly real they got hold of a dead dog and,
tying a string round its neck, they dragged it along
to a burial place. A group of grown-ups watched
the children, and as the little players passed each
grown-up made some disparaging remark about the
dead animal. It was a mongrel—a thief—an ill-
tempered beast ; but one young man, looking upon
the animal with gentle compassion, said, ' Pearls
cannot rival the whiteness of its teeth.' It was the
young Prophet of Nazareth (ah, did we not guess it !)
and so the witchery of his words went on. With a
long sigh we wakened up to find ourselves back
from the old heroic days when the Son of Man
walked the earth, yet He abides the same and He
still says to the playing boys and girls, ' Come unto
Me.' Mr. Morrison always ended on that note :
the living personal Christ."

Just after Dr. Morrison had left St. George's,
Edinburgh, to go to Thurso, an office-bearer
asked his children, as usual, where they would
like to spend their summer holidays, and the
reply came at once—" Thurso." Rather

astonished, their father asked them : " Why Thurso?" "Oh, because Mr. Morrison is there, and we will hear more of his children's sermons."

Another incident which happened in Elgin during his Moderatorial year :

He had been speaking to the children in the (then) High U.F. Church, and so gripped their interest and imagination that many of the children were obviously sorry to let the Moderator go at the close. But his spell descended most completely on one tiny girl who was found standing outside weeping bitterly. When the minister's wife, thinking the child had perhaps been checked or teased by some of the older children, asked what the matter was, the child between sobs replied : " Please, I don't want to go home ; he is such a nice man." In all his travels the Moderator can never have had a sweeter unsolicited testimonial than that.

How the children of the Sunday School loved his visit, and how eagerly they responded when he asked them to send in stories or accounts of their holidays ! Then what lively rivalry there was annually for the finding of the first coltsfoot, and the pencils given to the first six who were successful. I well remember one spring Sunday afternoon hearing a wild rush of footsteps up the Gardens. This was a race between two boys who had met near the Manse and were each eager to get to the door-bell first with their coltsfoot !

How he revelled in the quaint answers of the Primary children to his questions, and how eager they were to tell him interesting facts about themselves, their holidays and their homes. He had a quite marvellous gift of memory for children's ages and names, and each child in the congregation at baptism was put on the Cradle Roll and every birthday until the fourth it received a birthday card. After that they were supposed to go to the Primary School. If any child was sick or confined to the house it invariably received a post card from the Doctor, very often one ornamented by his own drawings of tiny people. For such a thing he had a perfect genius.

During his last holiday spent at Biggar he took the keenest interest in all details regarding farm and animal life, and only the month before he died he started a Nature Competition on the *Record* cover for the children of the congregation.

On Christmas Day he always attended the Christmas dinner given by the congregational children to the cripple children of East Park Home, and after the brief but joyful service which he always conducted he would be busily engaged serving out soup, steak pie, plum pudding and sweets to the apparently insatiable appetites of the children. All this was undertaken with such enthusiasm and real enjoyment. Only the last Christmas he was with us he spoke to the children on the subject of Jesus as the Lamb of God, and afterwards he composed a short hymn which was set to music by the late Madame Ada Crossley (a dear personal friend), and it was sung by the children to whom it was dedicated the first Christmas Day after his death :

THE LAMB

Jesus was Little ; his crib was a stall.
Jesus was Active, to rescue us all.
Jesus was Meek ; from all pride He was free.
Jesus was Bruisèd for you and for me.

Praise to the Lamb Who was spotless and pure.
Praise to the Lamb Who the Cross did endure.
Here let us give Him our praise and our love,
And one day we'll meet Him in Heaven above.

He simply could not resist smiling or speaking to every child he met, and it did not matter in the least to him if the child was a wee, bare-footed urchin, dirty-faced slum baby or a well-cared-for baby in a pram so long as he won some response. He came home one day and told me how in an East End street, while the rain was coming down in sheets, a little boy whose toes were peeping out of his ragged shoes stopped him and said : " Please, Minister, will you tie my shoe-lace ? " and there in the wind and rain he put down his umbrella, and stooping, did as the boy requested.

One morning after breakfast two daughters of a Wellington Church member were counting the tea-leaves in their cups, repeating at the same time a child's rhyme. One leant over to the other and said : " My cup tells a stranger is coming to-day—wonder who it will be ? " After thinking a little the other replied : " I know who it is—Dr. Morrison." " *No*," came the emphatic reply, " Dr. Morrison is *no stranger*." This shows how the minister was regarded by the little ones.

In his visits to hospitals, nursing homes and institutions he never passed through the wards without speaking to or playing for a few minutes with the children, and one beautiful incident which happened shortly before his death was as follows :

He had stood in a ward speaking to a little boy who was very ill, and after saying a few encouraging words of farewell he left the bedside, but before he reached the door of the ward the boy's mother arrived, and, full of excitement, the child said : " Quick, mither, look ! That is Dr. Morrison ; he has been speaking to me, and if Jesus is like him I'll no be feart to dee."

He had a great love for all dumb creatures. There were always one or two cats in the manse, preferably black, two special favourites being named Timothy and Peter. The usual thing was to find both of them enjoying the quiet and warmth of the study. No matter how busy he was, he would always rise and open the study door if a gentle " mew " was heard, and sometimes the cats found their way even into his sermons.

When in the country on holiday he never went out without having his pockets filled with lump sugar and bread. He fed every horse, cow, dog and hen that he came across, and it was no uncommon sight to see him crossing a farmyard or field followed by a miscellaneous crowd of animals. I am afraid I waged a constant war on him, declaring that my baker's bills were nearly doubled by his frequent raids on the larder, and I always knew when he wore an extra innocent look that he had just taken buttered scones or cookies from the tea-table. His first duty every morning—year in, year out—was to feed the birds. A large bowl filled with scraps of bread was placed every morning near the hall door, and no matter how stormy the weather was, before his own breakfast was taken, with overshoes on and umbrella up, he would cross to the accustomed spot, and if snow lay on the ground, clear a place for the crumbs, and feed the feathered family waiting in the trees. His great hope was that some day the sparrows would answer to their names, as in the Luxembourg Gardens in Paris. Most tenderly and delicately has this daily custom been described in a letter written by our good neighbour and friend, Dr. Boyd Scott :

" It is impossible to believe that we shall not see him again until we, too, pass through to that ' other

room ' which was so real a certainty to him. How
often have we, your neighbours, spoken of that
lovely morning ritual of his of emerging to minister
to the ' birds of the air,' of whom he had learned so
tenderly his Lord's gospel of trustfulness and *calm*.
The day was not well begun for us without that
significant little scene. We felt that it symbolised
that spirit which possessed him of communion with
Christ in the kingdom of gentleness and beauty and
childlikeness.''

AT long intervals (and I think this was partly
physical, and partly due to his Highland
ancestry) he would pass through a phase of
deep depression, causing him to feel that he
was not holding the Torch high enough, and
for these days he would be very silent, neg-
lecting no duty or courtesy, but absolutely
withdrawn behind a shadowed veil in his own
mind. The following copy of a letter which
he wrote illustrates this point :

" My dear. Your letter was like sunshine. On
Sunday evening I came down from the pulpit feeling
that I had failed—utterly, and could never preach
again. That makes me so wretched, as if I had
failed *Him*. And then your letter came, and the
birds hopped on to the branches again. You did
more than you know."

But these rare darker moods passed quickly,
and his calm, unruffled serenity would possess
him again. He had a very quick temper,
which was easily roused, but he had it well
under control, and within a few moments the

storm had passed. His nature was singularly young and child-like, and his tastes most simple. The so-called pleasures of life and society held no fascination for him, and his greatest pleasure and joy was to be surrounded in his own home by those he loved. Hospitable to a degree, he was never happier than when welcoming friends—or those who were lonely—to his home.

There was nothing *blasé* about him; in fact, he had a regular Peter Pan side to his character. It was almost impossible to keep up a feeling of anger against him, although, being so utterly human, he was at times very annoying. Sometimes when from physical causes or frayed nerves he had been cross or impatient, and would go into the study and shut the door, I always knew the course matters would follow. In a short time I would hear him call " Mother " and continue to call until I appeared. Then, putting his arm round me, he would say, " The brain won't act when the heart is not at peace ! You have been very tantalising and utterly in the wrong, but I forgive you freely." This was his invariable apology and plea for forgiveness. Then we both laughed heartily and the sun shone again. Perhaps, " very childish," people may say, but so we were, and our understanding and love never remained long clouded.

In a letter to a friend a lady writes of him :

" To a community of country women there was a memorable evening when he talked of Lady Nairne and her songs, and when, six months later, they learned he was gone, each listener knew she had lost a friend. I could tell, too, of a friendship which emerged from the desire of a child ' to know that man ' whom she had heard preach, of his weekly visits to an old saint who was not of his flock —surely ' the second mile '—of his courtesy to the maids in a home he visited, of the comfort his presence brought to a bereaved home when he himself was very near the point where the road began to dip into the valley ; all being enriched by a grace which must have been akin to the grace of Our Lord Jesus Christ."

He was very sensitive to beauty and ugliness hurt him, yet luxury was not necessary to his happiness. Books *were* necessary, but not books in fine bindings. His fastidiousness was always controlled by simplicity, and I think it was his love of nature that did that. The man who loved the sparrow and the coltsfoot could not be a sybarite.

There was another paradox in his nature, for with all his humble-heartedness he was very proud, and yet it was not ordinary pride that made him "cock his beaver with the bravest" and face life so gallantly. It was an odd mixture of shyness and self-respect, a shrinking from letting the world know the secrets of his inmost self, a high consciousness of what he owed to God, his fellow creatures and himself. And this combination of qualities made him at all times as interesting to those who study character as his brain and scholarship made him interesting to those who value mental equipment.

In truth his generosity of heart and mind were remarkable, and his appreciation of any service rendered him, or any other person's achievement, was always expressed in unstinted measure. The following post card illustrates this :

" MY DEAR FRIEND,

"Beautiful! That's what I call preaching. I really believe if I were to sit under you I'd get converted myself some day. You'll come again next year ? Friday, June 6th ?

"Ever,

"G. H. M."

L

His nature was far too big ever to feel jealousy of others in regard to pulpit work, and he was ever eager to have in Wellington the greatest preachers from every country in the world, and would often say that it was his ambition to let his people hear every preacher of note from Wellington pulpit before he left it.

I think one secret of the power and attraction of his own sermons to all sorts and conditions of people was the absolute simplicity of language and the individual note, also the sense of restful completion one got at the end. To the listener in the pew the sermon may have sounded simple enough, but it had cost the preacher much, because every sentence was weighed, polished, and put into a fitting setting before it was ever considered perfect enough for his listeners' ears.

I once heard somebody say : " Dr. Morrison's sermons sound simple enough, but it is the simplicity of a Parisian model gown. Let any home dressmaker try to copy it, and she would find herself in difficulties."

He was popular as a man as well as a preacher. His interests were wide, and he thought evil of no man.

The summer before he died he was invited to the annual inspection by the Glasgow Corporation of their Loch Katrine Waterworks. Surveying the gathering after lunch, he said to a friend :

" There's a face over there that interests me much ; introduce me."

" With pleasure, but you are as well to know that he is an agnostic " (after a pause) " also a bit of an antiquarian."

" Never mind the agnostic—introduce me to the bit of an antiquarian."

Which was done to their mutual pleasure and satisfaction, as both of them afterwards testified. The whole gathering without exception was greatly impressed by the short speech Dr. Morrison was afterwards called on to make, in which after some very humorous touches, he made a great appeal to them as fellow-workers for the social uplift of the masses of the people. In more ways than one the members of the Corporation showed they all held the minister of Wellington in profound respect. Yet people ask, " What was the secret of Dr. Morrison's success ? "

Those who knew him in his home as husband, father, friend and master, came under the spell of his winning and irresistible personality. Except when in indifferent health, or when some text refused to work out as he desired, he was always happy-hearted and full of humour and nonsense, and at times a regular tease. From the time he rose he always sang happily. He loved music and had a very quick and true ear, and a musical voice, and during the hour of dressing a regular miscellaneous concert took place— not at all times classical! because he loved the popular melodies and picked them up very quickly from his family or the gramophone. The songs he sang were like a musical barometer of his health, and I learned to dread the mornings when no cheery music issued from his dressing-room as an accompaniment to his toilet.

His kindness and courtesy to all who served him—either in the house or outside— endeared him to them and won from them devoted and willing service. The men who drove him regularly in taxis or cars, and the people in the shops he dealt in, all looked on the Doctor as their special friend. He knew all their family affairs and joys and sorrows, and although they had no connection with

Wellington, he was frequently asked for advice or to officiate at marriages or baptisms. Many touching tributes were paid after his death, and one chauffeur said to me : " Life will be much poorer without the Doctor." From those who served in the house he won the most willing and devoted attention. Nothing that was done for the Doctor was ever done grudgingly ; in fact, I used to tell him that he was completely spoiled. But in reality his was a nature that did not spoil, and it was because he gave so lavishly that he won such a full and spontaneous return.

No record of his life would be complete without a reference to the faithful and devoted service given during the last eight years by our old cook, Mrs. Houston (" Houstie " as she was affectionately called by the family and friends). " Houstie " was one of the real old type of family servants (who are, alas ! getting rapidly scarcer) whose whole time and interests were centred in her work and the family. She was a recognised character—a regular Mrs. Malaprop in speech—and I only wish I had time to recall many of her quaint and humorous

sayings. She reverenced and loved the
Doctor beyond words, but resented keenly
the many, and oft-times unnecessary, calls
on his time and strength, especially if they
came during meal-times. Often we would
hear her at the front door inquiring : " Have
you an ' appintment ' with the Doctor ? "
and woe betide the unhappy caller if he or she
could not admit that an " appintment " had
been made, or if no good excuse for the
call was forthcoming. To the unscrupulous
beggar she was adamant, and we used to say
she was as good as a detective for discovering
those who came not on legitimate business,
but to the folk and friends she knew her face
would wear a broad beam of welcome. One
day someone called to see the Doctor when he
was out, and her description of the caller was
delicious but rather misleading. She said :
" Doctor, he gave no name, but I think he
was a foreign gentleman, and he carried a
' mistaché ' (attaché) case and wore a
' slooche ' hat." As it turned out, the man
was very dark-skinned, but a respectable
Scot from Dundee ! Like her master,
" Houstie " was rarely flurried or out of temper, and no matter who or how many came

to the house she remained calm and dignified.
Once when the Earl of —— was to be our
guest for a night or two the Doctor, thinking
to tease her, said : " Well, Houstie, did you
hear that we are going to have an Earl as our
guest ? " Her quiet reply was : " That will
be very nice, Doctor ; I have served Earls
before, and I always found them very pleasant
gentlemen to get on with." I saw her pat
his Lordship on the shoulder when he said
" Good-bye " to her, but that he recognised
her worthiness was shown by the fact that
several times since he has inquired for
Mrs. Houston. A note such as I get
from her now and again is refreshing
and quaint, and is, I know, the result
of a strenuous and lengthy sitting, as
speaking, not writing, was her strong point.
She loved the morning worship, and always
at the end of the prayer one heard her
audible " Amen."

How truly were Emerson's beautiful lines
fulfilled in the Doctor's life.

" Do not keep the alabaster boxes of your love
and tenderness sealed up until your friends are dead.
Fill their lives with sweetness, speak approving,
cheering words while their ears can hear them and

while their hearts can be thrilled and made happier by them.

" The kind things you mean to say when they are gone, say before they go. The flowers you mean to send for their coffins, send to brighten their homes before they leave them."

I have never come across anyone who took such infinite pains in regard to every detail of his pastoral work, and yet these small details were the very marrow of his ministry and what made up the great and very perfect whole. He had indeed acquired " the gentle art of making happy " by his kind thoughtfulness, and all those small extra deeds, " the sweet doctrine of the second mile "—unmentioned by himself—were woven in with the larger threads of his daily labours. It was very rarely that a patient went into a nursing home without finding a few flowers and a kind message from the Doctor awaiting them, and, if he knew when they were returning to their own home, there would again be flowers and a card of welcome. He must have spent a small fortune yearly on flowers, but it was money well invested, as shown by the return of affection and gratitude he received through these twenty-seven years.

Frequently he would go long distances to visit those who were ill and wished to see him : sometimes people not his own members at all. On several occasions I recall him leaving Glasgow on a Sunday night after a very full day—travelling to London and to Leeds and returning the next night—to visit some sick person. He did everything willingly and ungrudgingly. I was the one who inwardly rebelled, as I knew well how he was overtaxing his strength, but I also knew that it was useless to object, as, where he saw duty, no one might interfere.

A story is told of how one day he had walked a good distance to see a retired minister in the country but found on arrival that the old gentleman had gone for a walk. The maid invited him in and gave him a cup of tea. A few days later there arrived at the Manse a parcel for the maid containing a book, and on the front page were written the words :

" I was a stranger and ye took me in."

G. H. M.

" One marvelled at his serenity. He never seemed to be rushed. He was quiet, one had almost said grave, in manner. In public he was invariably most dignified, but in his home he showed a gaiety of spirit which brought him to the breakfast table with some joke or whimsical play of humour in his conversation. Few men have their humour in commission so early in the day! And as he passed noiselessly in and out of his study, or received folk who came to him on all sorts of errands, he was always calm, apparently unflustered by extras which piled up in a day already planned to capacity with work."

He had the great faculty of never appearing hurried for time—an invaluable asset when sick-visiting—and he always gave to each person the feeling that they and their needs were his only thought and consideration at the moment.

Many instances might be quoted of his untroubled demeanour and behaviour in the face of unexpected happenings, but the following will illustrate what I mean. In 1920 he accepted the invitation of Bishop Chavasse to preach to the students of Liverpool University in the Lady Chapel of Liverpool Cathedral. He had not been reminded before entering church that before the sermon the words " In the Name of the Father, Son and Holy Ghost " were always repeated, and as he very rarely worshipped in an English Church, the custom had quite escaped his mind. When the congregation remained standing he knew something was expected of him, so he just waited for a few seconds, then quietly said, " Will you all kindly sit down," then proceeded with his sermon. Someone who was present told me that a smile passed over the faces of the whole audience, but the whole happening was so natural, they understood, and I heard that that evening's sermon made a profound impression on all present.

I have been asked times without number how he got through so much and yet found time to study. One had to live constantly with him to realise the quiet determination and concentration to the duty on hand— and the shutting out of every disturbing factor—which went hand in hand with every hour spent in his study. No one was ever allowed to be in the room when he was studying. He was extremely reserved regarding his work, and never read over any of

it to anyone ; and, if questioned in regard to
his text for the Sunday, would always give
that most exasperating reply : " Come to
church, my dear, and you will hear." Monday was to him a working day the same as
the others, and he rarely took any time off
during the week except on Saturday after-
noons, when for many years it was his custom
to take a long walk into the country, although,
as a rule, he would manage to pay one or more
pastoral visits during the walk.

People so often asked me what were his
methods of working—a question I found it
exceedingly difficult to answer, as I never sat
in the study with him except in the evening
when all the hard work for the day was over
and he was quietly reading. I know, of
course, that the great secret of his achievement and power came first from a heart
rooted and grounded in Christ, and a life
lived in hourly communion with God.
People always felt in his company that he
was constantly being renewed from some
hidden source, and indeed his roots went
down into the everlasting spring of water.
Another secret of his work was that he had
an extremely tidy, well-balanced mind.

Everything in it was used daily, and consequently there were no cobwebs in corners. And lastly, he was heart and soul in love with his work.

As I do not feel qualified to write on this question, I am going to quote what Dr. Morrison said in the course of an interview on his preaching methods some years ago :

" At the morning service I follow the old Scottish tradition and proceed along the recognised lines of expository preaching. People tell you this old idea must be surrendered to meet the demand of the time, but I feel it would be a tragic thing for the future of preaching if we abandoned this more closely reasoned and intellectually educative method, with its wholesome demands for severe preparation. And I find that our regular congregation, as distinct from the evening audiences which are of a mixed type, appreciate such solid diet. There are discouragements, of course, such as when a hearer comes to you, after a sermon into which you have packed your very best, and tells you that what he enjoyed most of all was the little story in the children's sermonette.

" These sermons involve long and concentrated preparation, especially as I almost invariably handle the greater themes of the Christian revelation at the morning services. This means the treading of well-beaten paths, and therefore makes a heavier demand upon the preacher's thought.

" In the evening my method is, of course, entirely different. There I allow myself a wider scope, presenting the Christian essentials in a somewhat different setting, and calling to my help every type of illustrative aid that may commend itself to me. I strive to give these addresses a strong human interest, my great aim being to win the attention, in honourable ways, of some at least of the vast class of people who sit very loosely to the church. The touch is naturally far lighter than in the morning, but this does not mean lack of preparation. I prepare as carefully for the one as for the other."

He was always ready to discuss both his aims and the means by which he tried to achieve them, if it was to benefit any of his friends, he was also ready to ask advice and never above learning from even those who were his inferiors intellectually.

He was never unkindly critical about others, but in regard to himself and his work there was a dour Scotch reticence and dogged perseverance, and a favourite expression of his was, " All I ask is to be allowed to gang my ain gait."

I know that up to the year 1914, his (Dr. Morrison's) sermons were fully written out, and read from the manuscript in the pulpit, but during the War he felt compelled to get into closer touch and sympathy with the people, and from then onwards he discarded his manuscript and spoke to the people directly. Except on rare occasions he did this ever afterwards, although he refused to be tied to any one method, and I have seen him, if the subject was an intricate or elusive one, demanding great exactness of expression, take his manuscript into the pulpit, but it was rarely read.

He used to say that he was not an extempore preacher in the true sense of the term, and up till the end his preparation was as careful and severe as ever, and although he had a wonderfully retentive mind which he inherited from his father, his notes were always copious and full.

In regard to his prayers, of which it has been said that they were always extempore but never unprepared, I have a large collection fully typed, and I know that they were all carefully and prayerfully thought out beforehand, and many a time he has told his younger brethren that this was the outcome of a lesson which he himself was taught during his assistantship in St. George's, Edinburgh. One day he was out walking with Dr. Whyte,

when suddenly in his very characteristic way,
the Doctor stopped, and turning to his young
assistant said, " Sir, do you prepare your
prayers ? " When the assistant answered
in the negative, Dr. Whyte simply said,
" I do." That was all, but it was a lesson
Dr. Morrison never forgot.

Another thing he often said was that he
could not understand preachers who said
they never read sermons, as he himself had
always been a great and interested reader of
them. In his own library, which numbered
about six thousand volumes, he had a considerable proportion of sermon volumes, including those of Spurgeon, Parker, Liddon,
Stopford Brooke, and the Scottish preacher
John Ker. Of the latter he said that he
considered him in some respects the finest
preacher we had ever had in the British
Islands, and for expository power, tenderness
and searching of conscience Dr. Morrison once
said " I know none quite like him." In his
library were also many volumes by American
preachers, and he used to find stimulus and
inspiration in them.

He was an omnivorous reader, nothing came
amiss to him with the exception of much of

our present-day fiction which he used frankly to say bored him, because so often not true to life, but he had a distinct weakness for good detective stories and stories of adventure, and often admitted their pleasant and tonic effect on an over-tired mind. Standard novels he read with real pleasure, and as a rule once a year he would take a course of reading some well-known writer of classical novels such as Meredith, Robert Louis Stevenson, or Anthony Trollope. He was also an enthusiastic reader and great buyer of biography, and generally read each winter one of the big poets, and had always one of Shakespeare's plays on hand.

To quote his own words : " Among great writers who have influenced me individually, Sir Walter Scott holds a special place in my affections. He seems to me the ideal man— courageous, chivalrous, sensible, sympathetic. He is the most Shakespearean personality of all our writers. I like the story of how his daughters were asked if they had read ' The Lady of the Lake ' and replied that their father only allowed them to read good poetry."

In regard to his collecting of books, I do not

M

think he followed any plan for building up a library (rather as he was heard to say, " I just let it grow, like Topsy "). With the exception of commentaries and other " tools " his reading was mainly general literature, and as he said his ruling interest was individual life. " I am almost as intense an individualist as Carlyle. Individualism is not the narrowing thing some thinkers would make out ; it is, in fact, that through which we enter into the wider life and interests."

I have notes of an interview during which Dr. Morrison said :

" I most affectionately urge my younger brethren to be constantly moving among the homes of their people. It is the great secret of a happy ministry. I used often to lose the happy freedom of Christian intercourse by the haunting thought that I must get a prayer offered before leaving. I do not worry about that now. I do not believe our Lord had prayer in every house He entered, but I profoundly believe that He never entered a house without bringing sunshine, help, encouragement and comfort—and perhaps conviction. If we could only do that !

It is not the prayers we offer when visiting that make the difference—it is those we offer before visiting, when we are alone with our Father."

It has been proved from church history and biography that a great preacher is not necessarily a great pastor ; in fact, it has frequently been shown that some of the most brilliant pulpit lights have confined themselves almost entirely to preaching, taking apparently little interest in the lives and material welfare or everyday interests of their people. I have spoken elsewhere of my husband's wonderful record of pastoral visitation, and during these twenty-five years have often heard it said that he was an outstanding example of the possibility of combining successfully devotion to pulpit work and preparation, and zeal in pastoral work. His preaching was only rendered all the more understanding, sympathetic and rich by the intimate knowledge he had gained of the circumstances and needs of his people during his constant visits to them as counsellor and friend.

Except in times of sickness or bereavement he did not make it a practice to read the

Scriptures or engage in prayer when on
pastoral visitation. Dr. Black, his senior
colleague in Wellington, used to tell the people
that they must not expect their ministers
to conduct religious exercises at their homes
as a regular thing, and that for two reasons.
First, because they could have no conception
of the deadening influence upon a man's
spirit which is the result of conducting
formal devotions eight or ten times in one
afternoon, and, secondly, because happy social
Christian fellowship and sympathy are ends
in themselves.

Professor Mackintosh, of New College,
Edinburgh, who for many years occupied
the pulpit of Wellington during the month
of August, adds his tribute to Dr. Morrison
in regard to his pastoral work :

" Though absent, Dr. Morrison never forgot his
people. At intervals, there would arrive from his
country quarters a note telling of friends for whom
intercession ought to be made, or asking that a
commendatory word should be said in behalf of
some Christian project for which the congregation's
liberality was to be solicited. His people, you
could see, were never out of his mind.

" That impression was strengthened by the
acquaintance with Dr. Morrison's character and

ways which I gained through conversation with many of those kind Wellington hosts who made me their week-end guest. It was easy to gather that he was regarded not only as a great Christian preacher, from whose lips his people could never hear too much, but also as the most thoughtful and devoted of pastors. He seemed to *think* more about pastoral duty than other men. The shepherding love that filled his heart was directed by unusually careful method."

Even when on holiday for a short time, such as a week's visit to London, he did not really rest, and generally several days would be spent going, sometimes long distances, to see any members who had been married, or removed to London or the neighbourhood. The fact of lifting one's lines of membership did not break his interest in his people, and wherever possible he kept in touch even after they had left Glasgow. This side of his correspondence was very extensive.

One very amusing but significant incident, brought to my mind by the Rev. Joseph Johnston, of Frognal, who was his chaplain during his Moderatorship, is worth relating. The last week-end before we sailed for South Africa was spent at Frognal, where Dr. Morrison had promised to take the forenoon service. The church was crowded, and when drawing near the close of his discourse, a telegraph messenger was seen to enter and to stand inside the main door awaiting attention. An office-bearer rose and interviewed him, with the result that he and the boy slipped out again and reappeared in the chancel behind the pulpit. When the sermon was concluded, and while the offertory was being taken, a reply-paid telegram was passed up to the preacher—along with a pencil· Dr. Morrison read the message, then whispered to the member of the choir nearest to him that there was no reply. The incident naturally excited a good deal of interest, and there was widespread speculation, after the service, as to the contents of a message that appeared to be so urgent. Some would have it that it must be concerned with " the King's business, which requireth haste," while others surmised that the Moderator had been recalled to Scotland to deal with some crisis of Church affairs. But although many "feelers" were put out by the curious in and around the vestry, no satisfaction was received. The midday meal in the manse was half-way through when Dr. Morrison produced the telegram, and in quiet, level tones said : " I suppose you would like to know what is in this wire ? "   The company replied in chorus that they would, so the telegram was handed round, and it ran : " Will meet you Monday, anywhere, any time. Betty." It transpired that a young lady from Wellington had, a few weeks previously, secured a post in London, and the Doctor, on leaving Glasgow, had promised her mother that he would look her up and assure himself that she was in comfortable quarters, and would report. He had written to the young lady the day before (Saturday), telling her that he was in London, and asking when and where it would be convenient for her to meet him.   She was so elated at the prospect of seeing her minister in the land of strangers, that when she found she could not get to Frognal to hear him preach, she at once dispatched the telegram, expecting it would reach him on Monday, but having prepaid a reply the wire found its way into the pulpit.   The incident has its amusing features, but is a striking illustration of the pastoral conscience which Dr. Morrison possessed and cultivated so diligently.

After every service—both morning and evening—there was a crowd of people waiting round the vestry door to speak to him. It varied, of course, in size, but I have often seen over thirty people standing there. They came from all corners of the earth and were of all nationalities, and the visitors' book, which lay on the vestry table, contains many interesting and notable names. To all he extended the same gracious welcome.

" One had only to watch him with the people who came in crowds to the vestry on Sundays to be aware that he knew how to handle folk. He made them feel at home with him, and with one another in the group in which they were met, and always with the added sense of their being associated together in God. He was gracious, but there was a certain aloofness about him. He was the ambassador of the Most High ! "

The morning service, as a rule, finished at twenty minutes past twelve, but he rarely left the church before one o'clock, and quite frequently it was one-thirty, or even a quarter to two, before he got home. The same thing happened after evening service, except in winter, when he had his class, or " Round

Table," immediately after, and very often it
was ten o'clock before he sat down to supper.
Sometimes he was so exhausted that I insisted on him getting right to bed and having
his supper there.   One great blessing granted
him was, that he could sleep at once and
quietly through the night, and in this way
his overworked mind and body found re-
newal.

He never spared himself, and no matter
how tired he was, if there was serious illness
or trouble, or if there had been a death in
the congregation during the preceding week,
he invariably went and held family worship
in the bereaved home before returning to the
manse.

" He literally lived for his people—so
intensely that some of us feel to-day that
he has died for them."

Whenever the subject of having an assistant
was brought up by the Session of Wellington
he put it aside, saying that he would like
to continue as he was until he had reached
the thirtieth year of his ministry in Wellington
Church, and then he would ask for a colleague,
or else retire. Besides, he used constantly
to affirm with a smile, " What   assistant

could do more for me—except, perhaps, preach an occasional sermon—than Sister Patterson, who is one of the most wonderful helpers any minister ever had, competent, tactful, understanding, sympathetic, and loved by all and, last but not least, patient and long-suffering with me in my worst moods." He was never tired of acknowledging his admiration and indebtedness to Sister Patterson, and after his going, no words could express the help and comfort she proved to his family by her affectionate understanding and loyal, willing service.

Four post cards sent to his Church sister when she was at a conference show how he kept in touch at all points:

10.2.25.

"To wait you and welcome you.   Hope you have a great time.—G. H. M."

11.2.25.

"Greetings.   The day promises well.   We shall miss you to-night.—G. H. M."

12.2.25.

"Good morning.   Glad you are having some sunshine.   We missed you last night.   Loving remembrance from me and many.—G. H. M."

13.2.25.

" Welcome home.—G. H. M."

Before each Communion season he always sent a little personal note to every member who was sick or who would be unable to be present on the Sunday, telling them that they would be lovingly remembered by him at the Table. Another incident comes to my mind of how he was brought into touch with a girl—a stranger to him—who was passing through a time of great mental strain and depression. To her he wrote a little note of cheer and understanding every day for nearly three months.

With the rapid growth of the membership, and the serious problem of no vacant sittings which constantly faced the seat-letting Committee, the Session decided to admit young people by profession only twice a year, at the autumn and spring Communions. As a rule, about thirty joined each time, and the Doctor kept a loving and interested eye on all his children as they drew near the age for becoming Church members, and sent out a note such as the following :

                              " 29, Lilybank Gardens,
                                      " Glasgow, W.2.
" MY DEAR MAY,

   " When the Communions come round, my thoughts
go out with affectionate longings to my young people,
and I write this little note to you, to say that if you
felt drawn to join the Church at this time, it would
be a very great pleasure to me to see you at my class
on Sunday morning.

                     " Believe me, dear May,
                         " Yours affectionately,
                            " GEORGE H. MORRISON."

His class for instruction met for three
Sundays, and after that he interviewed each
one separately at the manse.

   " I wonder how many people were taken
by surprise, as I was, when they called on
the Doctor before joining the Church. They
went probably expecting something in the
nature of an Inquisition, with searching
inquiries about their practice and beliefs.
Instead they were welcomed by a genial,
human man who made them feel at home
and at ease from the beginning ; yet when
they left the manse, they suddenly realised
that they had said far more than they had
meant to say. I hope no one will misunder-
stand me when I say that Dr. Morrison's

questions were always reverent and respectful. The consequence was that he always got a good deal more than he would otherwise have got, and most people realised after their interview, that for all its informality an occasion had taken place there also."

It was always a very solemn and heart-stirring few moments when, at the close of the pre-Communion service, Dr. Morrison addressed the new communicants, and then, while Mr. Turner played soft music, they passed one by one in front of their minister to receive their card and his handshake of welcome and blessing.

The week following the Communion, we always entertained the new communicants either at our home, or else, if the numbers were too great, in the Church Library, and these evenings, with their fellowship, good music and cheery games, will, I know, ever be a very happy memory to many.

HIS WONDERFUL MEMORY AND GRASP OF DETAIL

A faculty that he possessed in an almost uncanny degree was his power of remembering faces and facts about people, and birthdays and anniversaries often brought a little note, flowers, or some other remembrance. He apparently was taking no special notice of remarks made in conversation, or of dates mentioned, and yet his ear had been alert and his memory registering facts for future use.

The following is merely an instance taken at random, from amongst many others. A young girl who was just about to make her debut was taken suddenly ill. When Dr. Morrison visited her in the nursing home, he saw her anxiety to be well when the great social event for her was to take place, and he asked her casually what colour of dress she was to wear. On the morning of her great day, after she had recovered, she received from her minister a lovely bouquet of roses to wear, and the colour exactly harmonised with the colour of her dress.

Such little acts of careful memory made him the adored and ideal pastor of a great congregation. Someone in his study once asked him how he managed to get through and remember all he did. His reply was : " That was by a legacy of my dear father's method and good memory."

He always seemed to find time to listen to, and help others, and space forbids me to tell of the many who came seeking encouragement and advice, and to all he gave lavishly of his best. Students always had a very large place in his heart, and his gift of finding out lonely souls, and those needing the grasp of a friendly hand, was quite extraordinary. He very rarely lent money to anyone, but was generous to a fault in giving help, and one bit of advice he never failed to impress on young men, especially divinity students, was : " Avoid moneylenders as you would the plague."

Extracts from letters received by me :

" My first meeting with Dr. Morrison was at the Piccadilly Mission in November, 1904. It was the Communion Sunday, and I remained till the service was over, and was introduced to him at the church door. We walked up the street for about two hundred yards, when our ways parted. From that time I usually worshipped in Wellington on Sunday evenings, but I did not meet him again. In February, 1906, I was in church, and, as usual, sitting well up in the back gallery. The church was crowded in every part. After Dr. Morrison had finished reading the intimations, I was amazed to hear him say, ' Will Mr. Semple, a student, kindly come and see me in the vestry after the

service ? '   When I went round he greeted me thus :
' Come away, Mr. Semple.   I have missed you for
several Sundays, and to-night I thought you looked
worried and unwell.   I hope there is nothing wrong.'
I explained why I had been absent for several
Sundays, and said that though I was not quite well,
there was nothing to worry about.   (I thought it
would be too bad to tell him that I was greatly
worried over the failure of my memory, and that
my University work was suffering in consequence.)
He talked to me for a while and sent me away
feeling a new creature.   Two days later came an
invitation to spend an evening at his house.   To
me the incident will always remain outstanding
and characteristic.   A casual meeting for a few
minutes in the street, and from that date one of
the crowd that attended Wellington on Sunday
evenings, an unknown ' fresher ' from the country.
Then, fifteen months after, picked out from the
crowd in the far back gallery, and ' I have missed
you for several Sundays, and to-night I thought
you looked worried and unwell.'   And I had
thought I was only one of the crowd ! "

" Nova Scotia,
" November, 1929.

" DEAR MRS. MORRISON,

" Your new task will mean a great deal to all of
us who were admirers, not to say worshippers, of
your late husband.

" I cannot resist sending you an account of my
first meeting with him.

" It happened in this wise.   I was a young man
in my latter teens, and an absolute stranger in

Glasgow, but I was armed with a letter of introduction to Mr. R. of —— Church. This was in
1906. One evening I made bold to call and present
my letter to Mr. R. The following conversation
took place :

" Mr. R. : Where is your home ?

" I : Newfoundland.

" Mr. R. : Have you any friends in Glasgow ?

" I : None at all.

" Mr. R. : Do you intend to join my church ?

" I : I have not yet made up my mind as to what
Church I shall connect myself with, but I am
really a Presbyterian.

" Mr. R. : Well, then, in that case I do not think
I shall trouble to read this . . .

and I was shown to the door, my letter of introduction unread.

" Shortly afterwards I worshipped one evening
in Wellington Church and became a regular worshipper at the evening service. A few weeks later,
Dr. Morrison announced the opening of his Bible
Class. I remained for the class, and at the close
Dr. Morrison spoke with me on the way out. He
asked about my home in Newfoundland, and then
said: ' I have noticed you in church on Sunday
evenings and as you are always alone, I thought
you must be a stranger.' I have never forgotten
the gracious manner and the friendly words, almost
the first friendly words spoken to me in that great
city, and the final parting on that memorable night.
' Well, Mr. Wright, I do not know how it is in your
case, but in my student days money was often
scarce, and the men had to go without things. If

N

ever you need books, send me a post card, and my
church officer will bring them to your door.' Nearly
a quarter of a century has passed since then. I
came to number my friends in Glasgow by the
score, but the years only served to deepen the warm
affection and admiration I had for Dr. Morrison
which were born on that October evening in 1906."

In a volume of sermons, entitled "The
Weaving of Glory," one address is on the
text, "The God of Abraham, Isaac and
Jacob," and the following story was told me
first by Dr. Morrison, and afterwards by the
one to whom it happened, and who is now
in his last term in Glasgow Theological
Training College.

He says : "The Weaving of Glory " had
been given to me by my mother, and during
the War I had it on board ship with me,
and read a sermon every Sunday evening,
especially liking the one on "The God of
Abraham, Isaac and Jacob," Dr. Morrison's
divisions being : (1) The God of the individual.   (2) The God of differing personalities.   (3) The God of succeeding generations.
When the ship in which I was serving was
torpedoed off the West Coast of Africa and
I was left alone in the water, the thought
of the sermon on "He is the God of the

individual " struck right home to my heart,
and gave me a new vision of the individual
care of God. It brought comfort and hope
to me, and when I was picked up by Arabs,
and got ashore at Dakar, I determined to
serve the God of the individual Whom Dr.
Morrison preached, and devote my life to
trying to teach others the Love and Wonder
of the Fatherhood of God. That was the
turning-point in my life and career.

A typical letter written to one of his young
men on active service :

" 1918.

" MY DEAR FELLOW,

" I was glad to get your letter and to learn from
it something of your whereabouts, though dimly
and obscurely. But wherever it is may you have
the best of luck, and forget all sublimary wars in
the language of Eden. Hebrew always fascinated
me. I held a scholarship in it and had to teach it,
which is one sure way of learning anything. To
this day I always like to keep my Hebrew Bible
open, and find it the best of commentaries. What
a world of foolish unscriptural narrow theology we
should have been spared if Hebrew had been com-
pulsory. I am glad you are pushing on with your
Hebrew. There is no limit to what is possible if
a man doggedly and determinedly sets his face to
a thing. I have just been reading the newly
published life of John Brown of Haddington, one

of the great ministerial figures of the eighteenth century. He began life as a shepherd boy, and taught himself Greek and Hebrew without grammar or dictionary. It seemed so incredible that for years he suffered from the charge of getting his learning from Satan, and it was long before he gained admission to the Church. Some day I shall give you a read of the book. It is a rebuke to us in these easy times.

" Here I am in a tiny house with a tiny garden, and, what I have longed for all my life, a tiny orchard. There like Abraham I have pitched my tent—only his was of black hair and mine brilliant in its stripes—and there I sit through long happy hours wrestling my way through Browning. I take him up in my Class next winter. It's a great thing in times like these to have a big stiff subject to grapple with, and I do thank God these days that I have the habit and the joy of the student. With a son in France, and all the rest of it, picnics and the like are mockeries : but MIND holds the sceptre yet. So get on with your Hebrew !

" I can't *quite* make out the first word of your address, but trust this will find you. God bless you.

" To-morrow is our Communion and we shall not forget you.

   " Believe me,
     " Yours ever affectionately,
       " GEO. H. MORRISON."

To young preachers he gave this counsel : " Guard against the tendency to rush which is the bane of modern life. The habit of unprofitable bustle and rush, the present-day preoccupation with small affairs and engagements, is withholding many good things from us. For myself, it is essential that I have leisure to brood and meditate."

The only other advice he would give was that given to himself—as I have already mentioned—by Dr. Whyte in regard to taking good holidays. "That advice," he said, "I have always followed, and I have derived signal benefit. An adequate holiday is a *sine qua non*, not only for the sake of the congregation, but for the preacher's own sake."

With all his success, Dr. Morrison ever retained the modest spirit that will learn from the humblest friend, and never forget anything of any value that might be dropped by the poorest talker. To rich and poor alike he showed always the gracious courtesy of a Christian gentleman.

"No one who was with him could fail to feel that the man had resources in the Unseen, a deep that couched beneath, and what he said and did had an awesome power from what was behind it. He carried a hallowing atmosphere with him, whether in the pulpit or in more intimate intercourse with his people. Few ministers have impressed me as so entirely absorbed in their office. Everything that came within his reach he laid hold on for his one purpose. He was an interpreter to men of the life with Christ in God."

"There are twelve hours in the day," his life seemed to say, "time for all that is needed to be done. Therefore let us be quiet, unhurried, orderly, faithful in that which is least." But another note was sounded clear by that great life—a note of urgency. There are *only* twelve hours in the day. They must be filled full, full to the very brim, for the night cometh! And certain things have to be done. Above all, a gospel had to be preached, a message of forgiveness and love to the sinning, of comfort and hope to the weary and sad ones, and it was because he had time to know his people and to listen to them that so often his message just seemed to be meant for them."

Hannen Swaffer, the dramatic critic, in one of his series entitled "In Search of Living Churches," writes of a Sunday visit to Glasgow and especially Wellington Church.

" I was easily guided in my search for a living Church, because nearly everybody in the world of religion could have told me that Wellington Church of the United Free Denomination was famous all over Scotland, and that Dr. Morrison, its minister, was one of the best preachers in the country. I heard him preach in the morning, and although there was only a simple handling of the subject of the appearance of Jesus, I could understand the cumulative effect on Glasgow of a man with such a scholarly mind and such an honestly persuasive personality.

" He has no angularities of manner and he is anything but theatrical. Yet his preaching has influenced the whole of Glasgow and his writings on religious subjects, printed in more than a dozen volumes and regularly in the *British Weekly*, have gone all over the English-speaking world.

" When you see Wellington Church, which is immediately opposite Glasgow University, you think, seeing how its high Corinthian columns support a noble-shaped edifice, of a Greek temple in ancient Athens.

" I spoke to Dr. Morrison about this that night when I visited him among his thousands of books. I was trying to explain the ordinary man's attitude towards well-fed Christianity, although I did not mean him or his Church. I could understand a Martian, while passing that Grecian-shaped temple built on a solid rock of surety, with its well-clothed people confident in their faith, wondering what they were doing to solve the problems outside.

" Believe me, his first impression — one of

self-satisfied indifference—would not be fair. These well-clothed people, who went in to pray when I was there, seek to carry out practically what they preach. They do not boast of it. Yet in two mission centres which Wellington Church runs among the slums, literally hundreds of members of the congregation take part themselves, going down regularly among the poor, holding meetings like Salvationists, paying liberally. . . . They raised £225 the other Sunday, besides the ordinary collection for the church—and shedding sweetness and light.

" The influence of a man like Morrison spreads right across the world. In the University opposite are Chinese students, negroes from Africa, Indians, coloured people of every kind, being trained for medicine, for law, or for business. There come also Scotsmen from all parts of the Highlands.

" Morrison's simple eloquence stabilises hundreds of their lives. They go to Canada and Australia and India, and right across the world. This is one of the secrets of Scotland's strength."

The critic of Christianity may ask, " Why cannot Christ save Glasgow ? Why do not His respectable followers wipe out the slums and abolish the misery ? "

" More Wellington Churches and more Dr. Morrisons are wanted," is part of the answer. " It is not the fault of Christ or the fault of those who resolutely follow Him that the material world outside remain indifferent and aloof."

Dr. Morrison came of a family to whom teaching and writing were as natural almost as breathing. From his early boyhood his pen had been busy, and in the Glasgow Academy magazine, *The Academician*, his earliest writings were published. In 1883 he contributed an article entitled " Adventures on Ben Nevis," in which Mr. Gammie says : "There is a foreshadowing of the literary descriptive style and power for which in later life he has been so famed." Later on in the *Glasgow Weekly Citizen* there were numerous contributions in verse signed "G. H. Morrison," in which the music and poetry of his mind found expression. A line from one of these early poems, " A strange lone whisper fills the barren air," was chosen as the title of a painting of " Winter " exhibited in the Glasgow Art Exhibition.

Literary work always had an irresistible attraction for him, and it is not surprising that through his pen which he had wielded with such promise even in boyhood days, he should become known as an author ere many years had passed. One has only to scan the long list of his published works to realise how untiringly he wrote or how prolific his pen, and to remember that with it all his great work in the pulpit and congregation was carried on with unswerving fidelity and care. It was during his ministry at Thurso that he began to publish, his first book being " The Oldest Trade in the World," followed the next year by " Memoirs of the Life and Writings of Thomas Boston, with Introduction and Notes." This volume had many favourable press notices, including a lengthy review in *The Spectator*. From that time onwards very few years passed without some work from his pen and looking back, it seems to me that I scarcely knew when these books were being written, so quietly, humbly, and in such an unheralded way was all his work carried through.

During the last five or six years of his life congregational and other duties occupied his time so fully that he never saw his way to accede to the constant demands of his publishers for another volume of sermons, but he was able to bring out two volumes of his *British Weekly* articles under the titles of the " Gateway of the Stars " and " Highways of the Heart," and within six months after his death, the volume "The Ever Open Door" was given to the public.

" His books are now the possession of the whole Catholic Church. And an eminent English High Churchman once confided to the present writer that the sermons of ' your Morrison ' are more highly prized and more widely used than those of any preacher of our time, and he set them as classics beside those of Newman."

Yet no one was ever less conscious of producing classics than Dr. Morrison. One can recall his whimsical smile of deprecation when such a tribute was repeated to him or when he was asked for his " secret," as he often was.

Perhaps Professor Denney came nearest to that " secret " when he wrote in a review that Dr. Morrison had the gift of saying the things that we all would have said, had it occurred to us to say them ; and he said these inevitable things as we could not, in English prose that had the effect of poetry on the heart.

Sir William Robertson Nicoll, writing on this subject, also on the extraordinary saleable quality and success of his books of sermons, drew attention to the originality of his titles, and mentions a few—" The Anguish of the Light," " The Medicine of the Merry Heart," " The Tidings of the Breeze," etc., but many of his later titles were even more arresting, and at random I mention : " Have you Tried the Way of Love ? ", " Evangelising the Inevitable," " The Gladsomeness of Jesus," " Missing the Obvious," " Utilising the Incomprehensible," etc. Sir W. Robertson Nicoll went on to say that there is not a sermon in any of his books which does not deserve longer life than that of the spoken word, adding, " it strikes us that Dr. George H. Morrison has at least as much of the late Dr. Parker's gift as any other living creature." The following is a sentence taken from an address on the text, " Thou renewest the face of the earth "—Psalm civ. 30 :

" God never renews the human face by any kind of external application. God's beauty parlour is the heart. He pours new life and love into the heart till the face of the plainest woman becomes beautiful, and thus it is He renews the face of nature. Springtime is not an outward application. It is not anything added from without. It is the sign and sacrament of the new life that has begun to thrill within the heart of nature. Thus the old earth grows young again and the harsh lines of winter obliterated, and we rejoice in the miracle of Spring."

In 1919 Dr. Morrison attained the semi-jubilee of his ordination as a minister, and early the following year came the announcement that the congregation of St. George's, Edinburgh, had decided to ask him to become their minister in succession to Dr. Kelman, who had gone to Fifth Avenue Church, New York. I shall never forget the restlessness, uncertainty and conflicting desires of that week. The struggle for my husband was short and sharp, it was one of the great problems of his life. Letters and telegrams poured in from all quarters, pleading the counter claims of Edinburgh and Glasgow, and to add to the difficulties he had to be two days in London, had severe inflammation in one eye, and over the week-end we had some of the Cambridge students as guests, and occupying the pulpit in Wellington on Sunday evening. Once he saw his way clearly he did not hesitate, and his mind was at rest. His letter to the Moderator on the St. George's vacancy was as follows :

"Wellington Church,
"March 31st, 1920.

"DEAR DR. HARVEY,

"After much thought I have come to the conclusion that it is my duty to remain in Glasgow. For reasons which you know and appreciate, it has been far from easy for me to arrive at this decision, but, having reached it, it is final. Will you convey to my friends in St. George's my gratitude for this mark of confidence in me. I should gladly have let you know sooner, but that was impossible. I had little more than a week to make the most difficult decision of my life, and for part of that time I was in London. For all your own thoughtful kindness all through, I am, and shall ever remain your debtor.

"Believe me with all brotherly regard,
"Yours most sincerely,
(Signed) "G. H. MORRISON."

ALTHOUGH I have often heard Dr. Morrison say that Dr. Whyte never gave his assistants advice on any subject whatever, there was one exception to that rule, he advised them times without number to take good holidays, and years after when reminded of this, the old Doctor replied with a smile, " Well, sir, and if you have followed my advice, have you or your congregations ever had reason to regret it ? "

This was a counsel Dr. Morrison said he most religiously kept all through his ministry. But I doubt if other people would have considered that the time spent away from Wellington was altogether a holiday. He was always out of his pulpit during the months of July and August, but during that time he prepared much of his winter's work, his Sunday evening class work, any lectures that he had to give during the season, and he also did much solid reading. He breakfasted at the same hour in summer as in winter, and attended to his correspondence as usual, except that it was always considerably augmented by the sending of picture post cards to many members of the congregation. He was an excellent customer to the local stationer as he bought and sent off dozens weekly, always remembering those of his flock who were in domestic service, and sometimes, in little country village stores, cleared out their entire stock in the first few days. When the weather was fine he always spent a little time out of doors before settling down to work, but by ten o'clock he was as a rule busy, and, with rare exceptions, worked steadily till 1.15. If there was no sitting-room available for him to study in, I always tried when taking a house to have an extra bedroom which could be sacred to his use. He did not mind how small the room was, so long as he could have sufficient space for a comfortable chair and his large number of books. One of his most successful courses of Sunday evening lectures (on Browning) ever given, was prepared in Arran in a tiny attic-room with a skylight window. In the afternoon he slacked off till tea-time at 4.30, but if we were not going out for

any excursions or picnics he, as a rule,
studied again till seven o'clock. After supper
was the time sacred to our evening walk—a
custom we never allowed to lapse during our
married life, and which we always took alone,
unless we had visitors staying with us—and
to both of us that evening walk was a happy
and precious institution. From ten o'clock
till bed-time he was again busy with his
books.

Of course there were many days when this
routine had to be broken into, and no one
enjoyed picnics more whole-heartedly than
he did, but he preferred, if possible, to have
his forenoons unbroken.

One Sunday in the last week of September
we always took away together—our annual
honeymoon, he called it—also the first
Sunday after the New Year. Then at Easter
he took two Sundays off, and during that
holiday he prepared his June Monday evening
lectures, the foundations of which had been
gradually forming in his mind through the
winter.

" These June lectures were for many years
an outstanding feature of the Church life in
the city. People came to them from all

o

quarters, and many visitors from overseas carried away lasting impressions from those happy hours of study in Wellington Church. These lectures, delivered in the month of June, when most ministers are resting on their oars after the winter's work, were at once the delight and the despair of all Dr. Morrison's brethren. Many ministers attended them for the sheer pleasure of having the Word expounded by a master of literature and religion, and all of them were amazed at the inimitable freshness of the man. But not only ministers, but elders and teachers, and leaders of work among the young, as well as quiet souls in all the churches who love the study of the Bible, flocked to hear one who, with the erudition of a professor, could make clear paths through Scripture for the simplest learner. All found what they came for. The Fundamentalist and the Modernist sat together at his feet. For though no one was better versed in the critical work of the last thirty years, he had an uncanny way of leading his hearers through all the difficulties to the pure gold of the Sacred Word. He never lost sight of the fact that as a minister of Christ, his first concern must be how best to bring his hearer closer to the heart of his Lord. Hence the wide appeal of these lectures to the common heart. They were the outcome of his own private devotions in hours of leisure during his holidays."

A college friend, writing to me, says :

" Many a country minister who had been a little uncomfortable when he heard that ' Morrison of Wellington ' had taken a house in the village and would be worshipping in his church knew, however, a great sinking of heart when the holiday season drew to a close and took away the helpful, kindly companionship.

" During these holidays he was a regular and devout and most appreciative worshipper at the nearest church. During the week he would sail, drive or walk with the preacher, and would give or ask advice and be one of the most companionable and genial of friends. He had always some kind and encouraging word to say to the preacher about the services—either the devotions or sermon—and not seldom would say that he would have to preach some day upon the text that had been the theme of the day. It was generally supposed that he had a special ' flair ' for texts, but behind it all there was careful and constant study of scripture with every available aid."

Two letters written by the Doctor. while on holiday :

" My Dear ——

" Next to living with your friends is getting letters from them, for when friends write each other there is always a touch that sounds as if they were speaking. So you know how glad I was to get your letter and how glad to know that you were really better, and able to stand this thorny and workaday world again. I have often thought of you and wondered how you were getting on : but in remembrance of your absolute refusal to send me a card, had to content myself with wondering—and sometimes with something better than wondering, which you, and your husband and family, have a right to expect from your pastor :

" ' So the whole round world is every way
      Bound by gold chains about the feet of God.'

So you are going off for September. Well, remember I leave it with *you* to invite me out—suggest a few dates and I'll come. And on October 2nd is my birthday ; I shall expect a birthday cake, with fifty-three candles on it. And, by the way, will you send out a thought to me on August 15th—Friday next ? On that day twenty-five years ago I was ordained a minister—and I seem scarcely to have begun to preach yet.

" We are all well and in our own ways busy. How I love the long quiet hours of these summer days in my little study.

" Affectionate remembrance to your good husband —love to your dear bairns—and believe me,

" Ever sincerely,
           " G. H. M."

" My Dear ——

"It is Sunday evening, gusty, stormy, rain-driven, but with gleams of sunshine, and the birds singing as if life were a glorious thing to them, as no doubt it is. I have no doubt the Lord heard far finer sermons from them than He ever heard in the Synagogue, and perhaps the hearing ear does so still. What a deal there is in the Gospels that you only *feel* in the country and when you are leading the open-air life. I wonder if some beautiful summer Sunday morning I might not suggest to the congregation that we all adjourn to the Botanic Gardens and be still. I am so rested now, and at peace with all the world, and I want to be back among you dear folk again—as we will be by Wednesday.

" I am grieved you have been suffering, and yet were I to drop in just now you would suggest everything save pain—you paragon of brave deceivers !

" ' The mark of souls in making is capacity for pain,
And the anguish of the singer makes the sweetness of the strain.'

" It is quiet and beautiful here, and for the first time in my life I possess a tiny orchard where I have set up my tent, striped like Joseph's coat, and sit and dream and think my happy thoughts. I find I need rest and quiet. In front is the sea—round me as I write apple trees and the garden—and over all and in all—God. And if that won't rest my aching head nothing will.

" Here I build my rose-covered cottage to which I shall retire. But the roses are dream-roses and always will be, and dream ones are far sweeter than real ones. And they are thornless.

" Love to your dear household ; and to you my friendship.

"G. H. Morrison."

He was obliged after his operation in 1911 to give up golf, and had no other special hobby except field botany, but he never wearied, and no matter where we spent our summer holiday, he always found plenty to interest him in his leisure hours. Pastoral calling was so much a second nature to him, that even when on holiday, he continued visiting and interesting himself in all the cottage folk and children in the district, everywhere he went receiving a welcome. Pastoral work was never an unpleasant duty to him, and I have often heard him say that it was the crown of his ministry, adding, " I used to love books much more than people, but now I love people a great deal better than books."

His love of nature was an absorbing passion, and nothing escaped his keen eye. Every tiny wayside flower called for attention and admiration, and every bird and animal was food for thought, and generally found its way into some future discourse.

I remember how, one evening, in beautiful Glen Sannox, Arran, when climbing the hills, we suddenly came upon and startled a lovely young deer, and a few weeks later he preached in Wellington from the text, "He maketh my feet like hind's feet." I am quite certain that often when on the moors alone, or beneath the whispering pines, or under the shadow of the everlasting hills, God and he spoke heart to heart, and that he learned in these times of quiet communion the truths he later on from the pulpit imparted to others.

This intense love of nature was apparent through all his works and life. The titles of his sermons and his books seemed to come to him like birds on the wing, and who, looking over the contents in his books, can fail to be arrested and entranced by the poetry, originality and freshness of his themes and choice. The Rev. R. Barr, of Cape Town, in his memorial poem to Dr. Morrison, writes :

" The Spirit of Spring was in his mind
    As up and down the Book of Life he trod,
    New treasures in the best known parts to find,
    In darkest texts the rarest flowers of God."

As a companion on holiday travel he was

quite delightful and most interesting ; in fact, as good as any guide-book. Whenever his mind was made up in regard to the route or neighbourhood to be visited, he secured all possible good guides and books dealing with the history and interests of the places, and set himself in odd hours to get a thorough grasp of all essential knowledge. The result was that he went off on any holiday or travel thoroughly versed in all matters of interest, botanical and otherwise, and when travelling abroad this knowledge saved us much time. He really preferred to go to some place where he could settle down and have his books around him, but we had a number of most interesting trips abroad during our married life, including Italy, Italian Lakes, Switzerland, Holland, the Rhine, and Southern France, etc., and from all these countries he sent home to his congregation endless picture post cards and letters, showing how his interest and thought of them was constant and never-failing.

We also spent a delightful month in Devonshire in 1920, a gift from the congregation after his refusal of the call to St. George's, Edinburgh. With our wonderful tour in

South Africa I have dealt elsewhere, and truly, although a time of intense interest and pleasure, it could not by any stretch of imagination be termed a holiday. Always a keen walker, he used when on holiday to go for long tramps either alone or accompanied by some friend. He kept this up until within a few years of his death, when he seemed to grow much more readily tired and, I noticed at times, to become breathless. So after much consideration we came to the conclusion that as the family had now their own homes, we would be justified in running a small car. I learned to drive, and we found it not only a source of great joy, but also, when in town, a means of saving him much fatigue when visiting. He just loved the country drives, and the last Saturday before he took ill we had a drive out by the Blane Valley, that district so loved by him. Each summer the little car took us north to Nethy Bridge, and while there we were able to reach many lovely spots which without the car would have been inaccessible to us. One of his greatest joys in the car was the chance it gave him of taking people for a drive, especially those who by their work were confined in offices or shops, and when the long light evenings came we, or I alone, had the pleasure of taking many weary folk for a few hours into the fresh beauty of the country. He loved " the open " so keenly his sympathy went ever out to those who were weary and depressed with the daily round.

WELLINGTON congregation suffered the loss
of many of its finest young men during the
years of war. Over fifty made the supreme
sacrifice, and many families lost two and
three, and in two cases four members. At
no time during his ministry did Dr. Morrison
work harder or identify himself more closely
with his people than during these dark and
trying years. He visited untiringly the homes
where there was anxiety or sorrow, and kept
in constant personal touch by means of
letters, parcels, etc., with every church member on service. He also took a keen interest
in the welfare and movements of all the men
from the Mission districts, and every Christmas over 700 parcels were made up and sent
out from the church to all parts of the front.
He also acted as chaplain to Yorkhill Military
Hospital for some time, and in this way was
brought into close contact with wounded
officers from all parts of the world. During
the whole of this trying time he went about

his work with quiet and unruffled calm, preaching, visiting and travelling, and, no matter how dark the days or how depressing the war news, bearing ever with him a message of comfort, courage and unfaltering optimism that made living easier for all with whom he came into contact. These four years were a time of ever-increasing strain on body and nervous system, and, coming so soon after the very serious operation he had undergone (and the succeeding period of extreme weakness), told on his never very robust constitution, yet he never faltered or flagged in his ministering attention to those who needed him.

Then, one remembers that all this time in the background—yet never allowed to intrude between himself and his work—was his own great and personal anxiety on account of his two sons. The elder, George Herbert, was on a cycling tour in Germany and Austria-Hungary just at the time that war broke out, and although he made every effort to reach the frontier, was unable to get out of the country in time. After many exciting, dangerous and disagreeable experiences, he managed to reach friends in Mecklenburg-

Schwerin, to whom he had acted as tutor during a summer vacation a year previously. They willingly took him in and treated him with the greatest kindness and consideration until the internment regulations came into force, which made it impossible for them to keep him any longer. When he left these kind friends he was sent to the Civilian Camp at Ruhleben, near Berlin, where he endured much discomfort and privation, and, later on, suffered from serious illness which overtook him, along with so many others, until in January, 1918—when exchanges of prisoners were being made—his condition made his release imperative, and he was sent home to England.

Our younger son—Alexander Whyte (Sandy)—was only fourteen years old at the outbreak of war, but did whatever he could to help, giving up some of his holidays to make munitions, and as soon as he reached the required age in 1917, he enlisted as a private in the Gordon Highlanders. After six months' hard training in Scotland, and later a few weeks in England, he was sent out to France early in 1918. Almost at once he was sent up to the fighting line, and from then on until October was moved from one point to another, taking part in a number of attacks. He wrote constantly, cheery, interesting letters, and several times he expressed satisfaction that he had not taken a commission to begin with, as he said that, even after all his training, he felt utterly unfit for the tremendous responsibility of leading others into action. In his last letter to me, dated September, 1918, he said : " I believe my papers are now in the hands of my O.C., and although I would rather remain in the ranks a while longer, I know that Dad and you would now like me to accept a commission, and when I next get back to the Base I will see to getting the papers through."

On November 9th—two days before the Armistice—we received official news that Sandy was reported seriously wounded and missing on October 26th. Then followed a time of agonising suspense, during which news came to us only at intervals and in brief snatches. Finally, after many trying weeks, we learned that the little village of Famars, near Valenciennes, had been attacked and captured by the Germans, and that during the fighting Sandy had been very seriously wounded and placed in a cellar for safety with one or two others. Later in the same day the village was retaken by our troops, but when a search was made in the cellar for our wounded they had disappeared, and from that day it was as if a blind had been drawn down. During all that time of wearing anxiety Dr. Morrison went quietly and uncomplainingly about his work, never speaking about his own sorrow or anxiety except when spoken to, cheering, comforting and helping others all the time.

The news about Sandy was received by us first on a Saturday morning at breakfast time, and, handing me the official note, the Doctor quietly said: "Tell no one, and say nothing to me until my Sunday's work is over." His marvellous courage made it impossible for me to do anything but obey, and that afternoon we attended a large "At Home" given by one of our session to all our congregational collectors, and at it Dr. Morrison gave an inspiring talk on their work. Nothing was said about our anxiety to anyone, but after the news was made public it was said that everyone felt something tragic had happened to us. On Sunday the Doctor preached twice, and none in these crowded services guessed that he was speaking the message from a heart numbed with pain. The news was made public on Sunday night to a few. Then on Monday came the news of the Armistice and its following wild demonstrations. On Tuesday the great Thanksgiving Service was held in Wellington, and I shall never forget the strain and the tense nervous excitement of that hour. Looking back over these years of sorrow and anxiety, one wonders how human hearts and frames could stand the strain and stress of such times, and yet through these hours we were acutely conscious that we were being upheld by a strength not our own, and that underneath were the Everlasting Arms.

Although exhaustive inquiries and search were made no further trace or information ever reached us, and as months passed even the faint hopes of his being taken prisoner or suffering from loss of memory had to be abandoned.

In character Sandy strikingly resembled his father, and had in a great measure inherited his winning personality, thoughtfulness for others, tenderness of heart and quiet humour. He had not the brilliance of his

older brother George, but was a slow, perse-
vering worker. He had just entered his first
year at college when war broke out, and it
was his great ambition and full intention to
qualify for medical missionary work. Many
quaint and humorous stories were told of him
as a little boy at the Glasgow Academy, and
one especially amusing answer given to a
question in a General Knowledge paper was
as follows: The question to be answered was:

" Of whom was it said : ' In death they
were not divided,' " and Sandy's quaint reply
was : " The Babes in the Wood." How Dr.
Morrison laughed when Sandy with his attractive lisp retailed this incident.

Life must have been very hard for my
husband during those dark days of suspense
and waiting, as Sandy with his sunny-hearted-
ness and thoughtfulness for others was very
dear to him ; but he never uttered a word of
bitterness or complaint, and when asked how
it was possible for a minister to go on seeking
to bring comfort to his people while carrying
so great a sorrow of his own, his reply was:
" We have to consume our own smoke." He
had learned that " gentle art " in Dundee
and perfected its exercise through the long

P

years of his great ministry in Wellington.
" No one we have ever known had finer dex-
terity, through his great sorrows and in his
bodily affliction, in the art of consuming his own
smoke. His most intimate friends have only now
an inkling of how much there was to consume."

To a friend he wrote in November, 1918 :

" There is a heavy shadow over our home just
now. On October 26th Sandy was posted wounded
and missing. He has since been traced to a German
Clearing Station, but returning prisoners have
brought word that he was very seriously wounded
and not expected to recover. Frankly I do not
anticipate that we shall get good news now, and
indeed the bitterness of death is past. But Sandy
was such a splendid and good fellow, never causing
us an hour's anxiety, that whatever the issue be,
one can be certain all is well. Our news otherwise
is good. In the church things go on there much
as you knew them. My Browning Class is perhaps
the best I have ever had, and is full of interest to
me, and I think the Thanksgiving Service on the
Tuesday after the Armistice was the most memorable and thrilling hour I have ever had in Wellington
pulpit—not that there was any excitement, but a
deep and wonderful sense that every barrier was
gone and the whole congregation one in spirit."

Mr. Turner, our organist, writes me :

" A memory comes to me, and it is a sad one.
After the Bible Class was over one Sunday evening

Dr. Morrison turned to me and said : ' I am thankful that this day is over.' I said : ' Why ? ' And he quietly remarked : ' Sandy is missing, and I fear the worst.' It was such a shock to me that I could only say : ' I am very, very sorry,' to which he replied : ' It will be another bond between us, for you already have lost one son.' "

In 1915 Dr. Morrison, at the invitation of the Y.M.C.A., spent two months visiting and inspecting their work, which was then just at its beginning. His head-quarters were at Rouen, and the letter following will show how happy and interested he was in this new work which came to his hand.

" Rouen, 1915.

" I have really had a splendid time with the men, and now that I have got my bearings, I am able to hold five or six hundred fellows in perfect control while I speak to them on the War, Germany, or on any subject that comes into my mind. I do not know that I ever spoke better in my life than since coming amongst those fine fellows. It is quite a common thing when I have finished for some fellow to cry : ' Three cheers for the Doctor,' and then such cheers ! The authorities are keen to have me back here later on, and I am coming if possible.

" I have so much to tell but I am not allowed. How unreal and shadowy the life seems in Scotland. I mean how tremendously different everything seems when you are over here. I am very happy

and very well, and but for you, and my duty
to my church, wouldn't touch Scotland again
till the War is over.   It will almost break my heart
to leave.   This is living indeed ! "

In 1916 he had decided that if I was allowed
to accompany him he would return to France
for another short period of work.   I was very
keen to go as he said I could have assisted
him greatly by singing at his meetings and
in other ways.   Every effort was made by
various people in high places to get a permit
for me, but the restrictions had been so
increased all requests proved fruitless, to our
intense disappointment, and he would not go
without me.

It was Dr. Morrison's practice to have
certain Psalms sung to the same tunes at each
communion in Wellington.   They had their
association for himself and his people, and
helped to reproduce impressions made in
times past, and to create an atmosphere of
devotion.

He used to relate an incident that took
place during the War as justifying his practice.

One night somewhere in France, a company
of pioneers was repairing the front line
trench, and as the men went about their

work one of them kept softly humming a tune. A Tommy belonging to the unit that was holding the line approached the singer and asked : " What is that tune you are humming ? I know it, and have been trying to put a name to it, but can't." The other man was rather taken aback, but after considering for a moment he said : " Oh, that is a Psalm tune we sing in the kirk in Glasgow."

" Which church do you belong to ? " " Wellington," was the reply. " Put it there," said the Tommy, holding out his hand, " I belong to Wellington, too ! " and standing there in the glare of the Verey lights they gave each other the right hand of fellowship. The tune was " Boswell " to which the forty-second Paraphrase was invariably sung at the close of the communion service.

I HAVE tried to show how much Dr. Morrison
disliked the idea of standing in high places,
and it was almost impossible to get him at
any time to speak of his own work or achievements.   If anyone pressed him he would blush
like a shy boy and say: " We'll change the
subject, please."   Very frequently during
later years I heard people say: " Your term
as Moderator is coming near," and he would
reply with real concern: " Not if I can avoid
it."   But when rumours became more frequent and persistent, he braced himself to
face the music, saying, " I stand in a great
succession in Wellington, my people would
like it," and then, ever generous in his
appreciation and acknowledgment of my
interest in his work, he added: " And I
would love to make you the Moderator's
wife."   In 1926 he was unanimously nominated for the Moderatorship of the United
Free Church of Scotland, the highest honour

in the power of the Church to bestow. The city of his birth rejoiced in his new honour, and his own congregation generously released him from all pulpit and pastoral work for his year of office, so that he might devote himself entirely to the service of the Church at large.

This letter to the Very Rev. Dr. Phillip was written just after he had been nominated to the Moderatorship :

> " Glasgow,
> " November 24th.

" MY DEAR OLD FRIEND,

" whose name is forever intertwined with the memory of happy rambles, you make me your debtor by that kind letter. It is not only kind but in the highest degree helpful, and you may be quite sure I shall follow and profit by its advice. If there is any chance of you being in Glasgow during the winter do please arrange to stay here. It would do me so much good to have a quiet talk with you. I think this call is the most solemnising thing that has ever come into my life. I feel it, I think, even more than I did my ordination. It drove me to my knees. Do pray for me that I may be equal to all the duties, and that my strength, of which I have not a great reserve, may not fail.

" With our united, warm and affectionate remembrance to you and Mrs. Phillip,

> " Believe me,
> " Yours ever sincerely,
> " GEO. H. MORRISON."

The subject which he was led to choose for his Moderator's Address was one that had a long history in his mind. It was the subject of revival. For many years the sure hope of a revival that would be world-wide had been one of the basic certainties of his faith. A curious and significant thing was that the subject of the ten minutes' address he gave to the Assembly in 1897, on what is known as " Highlands and Islands Night," was in connection with a recent revival of religion in Caithness, and in his own notes he says: " This brief speech was, under God, decisive for my whole career. In a few days I was called to the pastorate of Morningside Church, Edinburgh, vacant through the election of Mr. Martin to a professorship, and though I declined the call, the conviction was born that I was not to be allowed to remain in Thurso where, up till that time, I thought my life work was to be."

In view of these facts it will not be surprising that he took for the subject of his address to the General Assembly " The Turn of the Tide—A Study in Revivals."

Some further notes on the subject taken

from his own letters may not be out of place at this point :

" Thank you once again for writing me in a way that gives me such real pleasure and encouragement. I cannot help feeling that the winds are beginning to blow, and that soon we shall have a spiritual summer-time as wonderful as that round us to-day."

Reply to a letter telling of help received by two casual hearers at an evening service :

" Thank you. These are the only tributes that mean anything to me. I do so earnestly want to be of help. Life is so difficult, and so many have never found the key that opens it. My heart yearns over them.

" I should like to say how deeply touched I was by the message you enclosed. Such things have been happening with unusual frequency in my ministry of late, and I humbly trust it is a sign that the words are both given and used. Perhaps one of the lessons we learn as the years go on is that we reach our best when we work a little less and wait a little more."

When one of his congregation was talking to her maid and fellow-member about the minister's longing for Revival, the girl replied : " Well, there's a revival every Sunday evening in the back gallery, if he only knew it." This was a little story that pleased him much.

A very full and interesting account of the peculiar circumstances under which the Assembly met that year, owing to conditions caused by the general strike has been given in Mr. Gammie's book, also details of the Assembly's one day sitting and subsequent adjournment, so I have asked the Rev. Joseph Johnston (then of Palmerston Place Church) who was Dr. Morrison's chaplain during his year in office, to give his impressions of Dr. Morrison in the Moderator's Chair, and other features during the memorable year.

DR. G. H. MORRISON AS MODERATOR OF THE GENERAL ASSEMBLY, 1926

When Dr. Morrison was unanimously nominated as Moderator of the General Assembly in November, 1925, it was felt that the United Free Church had done something that was waiting to be done. She was conferring the highest honour in her gift on one who was then her most outstanding preacher, and was making recognition of a ministry whose influence extended far beyond her borders. It was a distinction that Morrison had never coveted for himself, and certainly did nothing to invite, for he was seldom seen in ecclesiastical courts and took no active part in the work of the standing committees of the Church. But he accepted the nomination with deep humility and gratitude. In preparing himself for his year of office and the calls it would entail, he resolved not to discourse on the prospects of the approaching union, or to discuss problems of Church polity, but to continue to exercise his ministry as a preacher and teacher and to convey a message to the Church and the people that would make their hearts glow as though good news had come to them.

As the meeting of the Assembly drew near, there was confident expectation that in his address as Moderator, in the devotions of the daily sessions, in receiving representatives of sister Churches, in greeting distinguished visitors, and in giving God-speed to the outgoing missionaries of the Church, Morrison would rise to the occasion. That expectation was more than fulfilled. The opening address, which was a call to the Church to prepare and to pray for a renewed experience of Pentecostal power, was followed at the close of the Assembly by a complementary address on the congregation as the channel through which expected blessing would come. Both were memorable utterances that made a profound impression on all who heard them and quickened the pulse of the Church throughout the land. It was natural that one who lived in the atmosphere of revival in his own church services, and exercised his ministry so largely through congregational activities, should choose two themes on which he could speak with the authority of his unique experience.

The speeches he delivered from the Chair, when he spoke as the mouthpiece of his Church, were characterised by a depth of sincerity that redeemed them from formality, and were expressed with a literary grace that was his own peculiar gift. Two unique events took place during the sessions of Assembly, when the then Prime Minister, Mr. Stanley Baldwin, accompanied by Mrs. Baldwin, paid a courtesy visit to the Court, and again when three leading representatives of the Miners' Union, Mr. James Brown, Mr. William Adamson, and Mr. Robert Smillie, all Members of Parliament, were granted their request to present to the House the case for the strikers. On both of these occasions the Moderator rose to the height of his power and expressed the sympathetic interest of the Assembly with consummate tact and dignity.

There was widespread speculation when he was called to the Moderatorship as to how he would acquit himself presiding over the routine business of the Court. To those who knew him only as " a lover of quiet ways " who, outside his pulpit, his study, and the homes of his people, was believed to have few interests except in the country-side, his conduct in the Chair was a revelation of his capabilities as a master of assemblies. He was assiduous in the devotion he gave to his duties, following the reports and discussions with alert interest, and intervening only when it was necessary to speed up the conclusion of a debate, or, in consultation with the clerks, to settle a point of procedure. This he would do with a touch of genial humour and a gracious gesture of reluctance that preserved the happiest relations between the " floor " and the " chair." The fact is, that those who knew him best were aware that Morrison was no dreamer who loved the gates of Zion, but disliked the battle at the gates.

Witness the leadership he gave to his great congregation with all its agencies organised and working smoothly. He had a singularly orderly mind, with a power of detachment fitting him to intervene effectively in business and debate, while his sane outlook and balanced judgment would have made him a force in the councils of the Church. But he deliberately chose to limit the range of his active interests, thereby deepening the channel of his influence, and the course he took, and so steadfastly pursued, was abundantly justified by results.

He confessed that he " enjoyed every minute of the Assembly." It brought him into closest association with the leaders of the Church and its active administrators, clerical and lay alike, and nothing gave him greater pleasure than to recount in private unsuspected traits of character he had discovered in contact with them, for he loved his fellows and found peculiar joy in proclaiming them to be better than they knew. It may be that the " stir of camps " was a new enterprise for him, and when he saw the cavalry brigade and the footmen engaged in their annual manœuvres, deploying their forces, advancing and retreating, executing skilful movements and capturing strategic positions, the spectacle had its fascination for him.

He was unwearied, too, in the attention he gave to the social functions of the Assembly, and was captivated by the gracious hospitality he received at Holyrood, where the historical association of the Palace made a strong appeal to him. He entered with zest into the receptions given by Mrs. Morrison and himself to the members of Assembly and their friends, and he kept all his engagements with punctilious care and fulfilled them with unflagging zeal.

In all the functions connected with his office he carried himself with unconscious dignity, and moved from point to point, through those busy days and nights, with undisturbed serenity. Many met him then for the first time, who had long known him through his books and writings, and had felt his touch upon their spirits, and when they poured out their hearts to him in grateful acknowledgment of the debt they owed him, he modestly interpreted their words as a tribute paid to his position rather than to himself.

No detail was overlooked.   On the opening day of the postponed Assembly a mistake had been made by the hirers who sent, in place of the car ordered for him, a glorified taxicab, and it did not escape his notice.   He knew what was due to his office, and as he served his Church with his best, he expected others to do the same.   In this spirit, he graciously acknowledged the salute of the policeman on point-duty at the foot of the Mound, and with an apt quotation drew attention to the "serried ranks" of people waiting on the pavements for the Lord High Commissioner's procession, referring to his own modest display as "the false dawn" of the full-orbed glory following.

His opening address, which took the better part of an hour to deliver, was given without a note.   One would have expected him to have been preoccupied with the thought of it, but he gave no sign of the strain that was on him, and while he was waiting in his retiring-room for the summons of the Assembly officer, he talked with his chaplain of interests that were worlds away from the business in hand.   When the Assembly had closed, he gave no outward sign of fatigue, but those who had been closely associated with him knew that he had been renewing his strength from day to day at the source of power, in quiet moments, by the way. He left Edinburgh, to all appearance, as fresh as when he entered it, and returned to his home in the West, eager to set out on the tour of the Highlands and Islands with which his Moderatorial programme opened. Those who accompanied him on that itinerary, and on a similar mission to the Border churches, can tell of his triumphal progress, and of the train he left behind him of quickened congregations, ministers and office-bearers stimulated by his message, and manses sanctified by his presence. But perhaps, to him, the outstanding feature of his mission to the Home Church was the part he took in the evangelistic campaign in West Fife. It appealed to him as the work for which his congregation had released him for a year—to carry the evangel into the wider field. It was an exhilarating experience to this "spellbinder" to find himself confronted with a very different audience from which he was used to—composed largely of hostile, and even rowdy elements. But he gave

Q

conspicuous proof of his skill to handle men with the spoken word, of power to subdue their minds and hearts with his commanding personality, and to commend his Master to their conscience. The truth is that Morrison was, as we said of another, " a great human," and nothing that concerned our humanity was alien to him. He was not effusive, but he burned with a fire that was banked to last, and he moved among men, a radiant spirit, kindling others with his own glow. He could not but prove a great Moderator, because he was great in himself—greater even than anything he accomplished.

MEMORIES OF SOUTH AFRICA

IT had always been one of my most cherished dreams to visit South Africa, but more especially to visit some of our Missions in that country, and I shall not easily forget the thrill of excitement that passed over me when the proposal was made that Dr. Morrison and I should spend the last four months of his year of office, visiting some of the Presbyterian churches, also some of the mission stations of the (then) United Free Church in South Africa.   Former Moderators had visited Italy, Hungary, and other European countries, but Dr. Morrison established a precedent when he willingly agreed to travel such a distance, and undertake such a difficult and strenuous visitation in so short a time.   When the proposed visit of the Moderator became known, requests poured in from all parts of South Africa, and indeed from mission stations and churches far

beyond the bounds of possibility in regard
to time and distance, and those in authority
empowered to make arrangements for our
journey had a difficult task, so many requests
had to be refused, and so much considered,
so that our all too brief time might be spent
to the very best advantage.

The itinerary drawn out for us was very
comprehensive and most magnificently
worked out, and we were often lost in admiration as the arrangements in our intricate
journeyings fitted in each day like a jig-saw
puzzle, nevertheless, Dr. Morrison frequently
told audiences that those responsible for our
itinerary, also the folk in South Africa,
evidently thought the constitutions of their
visitors were not only made of iron, but of
reinforced concrete.

From the moment we landed at Cape Town
on February 21st, until the day we sailed for
England, on May 6th, we never once required
to look up trains, or consider ways and
means. We knew exactly the minute of
departure and arrival on every stage of the
tour, and except for a few mishaps during our
tour by motor through the Transkei, caused
by unforeseen circumstances, everything

happened as planned.   We had only to obey and " keep on going on," Dr. Morrison's favourite quotation.   The fact that Dr. Morrison was the first Moderator in office to visit South Africa, also that his name through his books and the *British Weekly* was known and loved, assured him of a warm welcome from multitudes who had never met him, but had considered him as their spiritual teacher for years, and from the moment we landed at Cape Town until we re-embarked ten weeks later, we received everywhere a welcome and hearing that it would be difficult to describe fitly.

Although our visit to South Africa was in more than one sense a great success, and we had reason to believe a blessing to many, there is no doubt that it was a great strain on the Doctor physically.   From the date of our return, until his death fifteen months later, I was very conscious that his work was more of an effort to him, that his power of endurance was lessened, and that more rest was necessary.   He had always to be very careful of his diet, and this, of course, was impossible to observe when travelling as we did, under all kinds of difficult conditions and with the fatigue of constant travel, excitement, and climatic extremes to face.

Never was my faith more sorely tried than on various occasions during that tour, as for instance, when during one night, on our train journey through the Kalahari Desert to Victoria Falls, he was seized with severe pain. I tested then the feeling of the helplessness of man when faced by such a contingency, and of our utter dependence on a loving Father. Mercifully the danger passed, but I had many anxious hours and on a tour such as ours, with practically every moment planned out, there was no allowance made for unarranged happenings. I always felt quite sure that we were meant to fulfil and carry out that tour, and that God was guarding us all the way through, as only once had we both to call off an engagement.

This letter was received the year previous to his Moderatorship :

" Bulawayo,
" Rhodesia,
" 1925.
" DEAR DR. MORRISON,

" It has been my privilege to visit various place in Southern Rhodesia during the last few months, and I feel I ought to tell you that on several occasions

I have found good Christian families living in the solitary wilds who regard you as their only minister. One such I found a few months ago at a place called Matesi near the Victoria Falls and about 280 miles from my own church to the north-east, and I am the nearest Presbyterian minister.

" The old man, a farmer, holds a religious service in his home every Sunday afternoon, and reads your sermon in the *British Weekly*. I visited another farmer a fortnight ago, at a place called Adzi, near the Portuguese border, 470 miles north-west of Bulawayo. This man is a modern edition of Burns's cottar. Morning and evening he takes the Book, the Psalms of David being sometimes accompanied by the howling of baboons in a neighbouring kopje. On Sunday he holds a regular church service, when your sermon is read and, no doubt, in the good old Scotch way, discussed afterwards.

" I thought that if anyone appreciated my sermons like that, I should like someone to tell me. So I decided to send you this note.

" With brotherly greetings and good wishes.
" Very sincerely,
" ALLAN MUNN."

We had a delightful voyage out, our only stop being at Madeira, where we went ashore and had breakfast with Mr. Purves, our minister at Funchal, afterwards visiting his pretty little church which stands amongst great palms and other tropical trees.

Lady Haig, who was recovering from

illness and going out to stay with friends, and at Government House, sat next to us at table, and we learned to have a real affection for her with her delightfully frank and amusing charm. She and the Doctor had many friendly battles and arguments over literary matters and deck games. When she learned that I was writing his life she sent me the following kind letter. Our visit to Bemersyde which she refers to, took place only two weeks before the Earl died, in fact, I think we were the last guests of the great Field-Marshal at his historic and lovely home.

" Bemersyde,
" St. Boswells,
" January 19th, 1930.

" Dear Mrs. Morrison,

" I shall never forget that pleasant journey to South Africa in February, 1927, when I met Dr. Morrison. As you remember, I was travelling by myself, recovering from a serious illness. It is a very lonely thing to be on board a big ship when most people have someone travelling with them, and all are joining in games and enjoying themselves, but Dr. Morrison and you, who were going to tour South Africa in connection with his work as Moderator, showed me such kindness as made the whole difference to my voyage.

" I was much struck by Dr. Morrison's simplicity of character, and humour, and during meal-times he would bring out the most amusing remarks, especially as we had a delightful young honeymoon couple sitting beside us. All who met him must have felt what a truly kind man, though such a learned one, Dr. Morrison was.

" He took part in all the games and interests on board ship and showed wonderful skill at deck quoits. I used to have great fights with him, but in the end he usually won. During our games and in conversation, the remarks he made so kindly, and later on the beautiful little book on ' Hope,' were the greatest help to me during my trouble which came so soon afterwards. I also recall the happy visit you both paid us at Bemersyde shortly before my husband's death. I did so admire Dr. Morrison and shall never forget him.

" Like my husband, he was so simple, although such a big man.

" Affectionately yours,
" DOROTHY HAIG."

It had been arranged that we should travel to Kimberley by the Union Express immediately after our arrival at Cape Town, but the evening before landing a wireless message reached us on the *Windsor Castle* saying, " Presbytery greetings, deputation on board 8.45 a.m. to-morrow. Mayoral luncheon ; expect short address for publication." So this meant the changing of our first day's plans.

Very early on the morning of the seventeenth day after leaving Southampton, in brilliant sunshine and intense heat, we entered Cape Town harbour, and by nine o'clock a large company of ladies and gentlemen representing the Church and town came on board. We held a regular reception and had a wonderful welcome.

The Mayor's car was placed at the Moderator's disposal for the forenoon, and I was taken in charge by the ladies of the party. Both cars took the same route to begin with, and we had a very lovely drive round that most wonderful coast road to Hout Bay, where we all had eleven o'clock tea under the trees. The Mayor gave a luncheon to the Moderator at the Town Hall, and I was the guest at a ladies' luncheon given at the Mount Nelson Hotel.

At three o'clock we all met again at the station, and before boarding the train we were presented with a magnificent basket of fruit for the journey. We chanced to land at Cape Town on one of the hottest days for two years, the temperature in early morning was 102 in the shade, so in more ways than one we had a very warm reception.

Having missed the Union Express by stopping at Cape Town, we were obliged to take the slow train, travelling through the dusty Karoo in intense heat, and we were thankful to reach Kimberley next evening, having ascended nearly 4,000 feet in a journey of 664 miles.

At Kimberley, where we only stayed one night, we fulfilled a number of engagements and visited the De Beers Diamond Mines. Our next visit was Bloemfontein.

During the short train run we passed through a sand-storm. It did not last long, but penetrated into everything, and when over, left us feeling as if eyes, ears and mouth were filled with sand.

The train was specially stopped at a level crossing, where we and our luggage were deposited. Our host, Mr. Murray (a Caithness man), met us with two cars, and drove us a short distance to his lovely bungalow on the veld, where we were to stay till the next night. In the evening we motored the five miles into Bloemfontein to a mayoral reception. The Caledonian Society of that town have a fine pipe band, and they met us about a hundred yards from the Town Hall, where we dismounted from our car and marched up the street to the music of their pipes amid admiring crowds of every colour under heaven. To hear the pipes playing Highland music in the heart of Africa was so touching that I was glad that I was not called on to speak for some little time.

During the following days we visited beautiful and interesting Pretoria, then Johannesburg.

Wherever we had been since landing, we had felt quite at home amongst Scottish folk and surroundings, but at the Mission Church at Johannesburg, when we stepped that Sunday afternoon through a door on to a platform, and found ourselves face to face with a large congregation composed entirely of coloured people—men, women and children— and took part in the impressive and touching service, it made us realise the wonderful work the missionaries were doing.

We were introduced by the Rev. Mr. Gardiner, and all we said was interpreted by two natives into different languages (for the natives speak many languages). After this there was a prayer in Kafir, and a hymn sung with great spirit and tunefulness. The

Moderator gave a short address, and I spoke briefly to the women. This was the first time we had spoken to a native audience, but we found that if we spoke very slowly and used simple language, it was neither embarrassing nor difficult, and we quite enjoyed our first native service. The whole congregation sang the Lord's Prayer, then a hymn to the tune " Sun of my soul." At the conclusion we shook hands with a large number of native elders, evangelists, and women workers, some of whom in English spoke kind words of welcome and appreciation of our visit to them. The entire congregation waited to see us drive away, all the men respectfully standing with their hats off. I just wished that the people at home who say they do not believe in Foreign Mission work could have taken part in that service.

During the two and a half days' stay in Johannesburg we both fulfilled many engagements, church and social, but I was allowed time one forenoon, while the Moderator attended a Presbytery meeting, to go with a party to see over one of the gold refineries. This was a most interesting and wonderful visit, but space forbids me to give a full account of all we saw and learned from it, and in truth the statistics in regard to output, daily and yearly, values, etc., made my brain reel. I only remember that small bars of gold which we were allowed to handle (but not to keep) were worth seventeen hundred pounds each.

Travelling is wonderfully comfortable on South African and Rhodesian railways. You live and sleep in your own compartment (and through the courtesy of the railway company we had a reserved compartment throughout our tour), and have your meals in the dining car, where the food is very good and moderate in price. Coffee is brought to you at 6.45 a.m., and fruit, sweets, ices, etc., are brought round at intervals during the day. We were fortunate in having rather dull, moist days for our long train run to the Falls, and so escaped the great heat and dust of the Kalahari Desert.

Although it added greatly to the length of our journey, it had been arranged that we should spend three days at the Victoria Falls, and we were very glad that this most wonderful beauty and experience was made possible for us.

The Falls station practically adjoins the

hotel. Our room opened on to the terrace, and all day long we could see the clouds of spray rising from the gorge. We spent a quiet forenoon on the day of our arrival, and after tea went down in one of the little trollies to the bridge, from which we had our first view of the Falls. Although they can only be seen in parts and at intervals, because of the dense volume of spray which rises constantly, they are so awesome in their grandeur and vastness that words cannot describe their magic beauty. There are many viewpoints, the best being from the Rain Forest, a place you can only investigate if clad in oilskins, as the moisture there falls like a heavy thunder rain and quickly soaks one to the skin. This we visited before breakfast on Saturday.

Sunday was an exceedingly hot and very exhausting day. A church service had been arranged in the town of Livingstone, six miles distant on the other side of the river. We took the trolly to the bridge, walked across, and were met on the other side by a gentleman who drove us to Livingstone for the service.

Livingstone, the capital and administrative

head-quarters of Northern Rhodesia, is a charmingly situated little place, with about a thousand of white population. The surrounding country is very like some of our pastoral English districts, but it is oppressively hot at some seasons. There is no Presbyterian church, and the service was held in the Court-house, which had been graciously granted by the Governor. Five hundred bills had been printed, but not all distributed, as the natives, unwisely being paid in advance, had only delivered a few and destroyed the rest ; consequently the congregation was very small, numbering about forty, and a dog ! After lunching with one of the leading men of the place, we returned to the hotel and spent the rest of the day quietly.

At Wankie, a great coal-mining centre some hours south of the Falls, we had promised to occupy the twenty minutes' stop motoring round the mines. Mr. Thomson, the manager, was waiting beside the line with his car, and in spite of the train being ten minutes late, on receiving a promise from the station-master that he would keep the train waiting for us for fifteen minutes;

we were rushed round the place in a way that left us quite dizzy. We saw, in our wild rush, something of the pit-working, the European and native quarters, the natives coming off the day shift, and receiving their rations, and various other interesting things. We then raced back across the line, still in the car, in front of our waiting train, and climbed on board, breathless and almost speechless from our rapid flight.

The Wankie mines, which are said to possess enough coal to last two thousand years, are producing three thousand tons a day, most of which goes to the Belgian Congo.

During our stay at Salisbury we were the guests of the Hon. Howard Moffat, Minister of Roads and Mines (since made Premier of Southern Rhodesia), and one of the famous missionary family. It was a great joy to spend two days in his quiet, beautiful home after so much travelling. One forenoon we went with our host and hostess to Government House, where we were guests for luncheon of the Governor, Sir John Chancellor (one of the family whose home for centuries was Shieldhall, Biggar, Lanarkshire). Government House, with its spacious, cool stoep and

R

lofty rooms, is a very attractive home, and we thoroughly enjoyed our visit. Later on in the afternoon I addressed a large meeting of women, and in the evening there was a civic reception at which the Governor and his staff were present. We had church engagements the next forenoon and evening, but in the afternoon had a most enjoyable visit to a typical Rhodesian farm owned by a Campbeltown man who has wonderful herds of Angus and other breeds of cattle. About thirty friends from the neighbourhood were asked in to meet us at tea.

From Salisbury we returned again to Bulawayo, where the nine hours of our visit were again crammed full with engagements. Immediately after breakfast we started by car to visit the Matopos Mountain and Rhodes' grave, a drive of twenty-eight miles through wonderful scenery. The " World's View," as seen from Rhodes' resting-place on the mountain top, is one of the most impressive and magnificent views I have ever seen, and we regretted our time there was so short.

Passing south through Natal on our way to Durban, we stopped at Glencoe. Rain began to fall heavily just after our arrival,

and continued all night, and we wakened to
a rainy and wind-swept scene, reminding us
of a wet stormy July day at home The
prospect of a ninety-mile drive in an open
car under such conditions and over inde-
scribable roads was not inviting, but we had
stopped at Glencoe on purpose to drive out
and visit the Gordon Memorial Mission, and
would have felt very mean to allow the
weather to deter us, so at 9.45 we set out
on our long, wet drive. The drive for pure
discomfort baffles description. We took four
and a half hours to do the outward journey,
the rain growing steadily worse as we proceeded until we were all pretty well soaked,
as South African rain laughs at the so-called
protection of waterproofs, and ere long a
steady trickle of water fell from various
points of the hood of the car. In spite of
chains on the wheels of our car, we had to
crawl most of the way, the car indulging in
an almost incessant series of skids, and more
than once we thought we were right over
on our side. A few miles from the mission
we left the main road and began to jolt over
fields and rocky tracks, until I felt the car
must come to pieces. We arrived at the

mission at 2.15 instead of noon, very weary,
damp and chill, and after a hurried lunch
proceeded to the church, where, in spite of
awful weather conditions and the long wait,
fully four hundred natives and scholars were
assembled.

The Gordon Memorial Mission is under the
control of a joint committee of our two
Scottish Presbyterian Churches, and was
founded in memory of a brother of the Earl
of Aberdeen, who died at Oxford when about
to proceed as a missionary. The mission is
in charge of Mr. Matheson, whose son we had
already met at the native church in Johannesburg.* The Moderator and I spoke through
the aid of an interpreter, and were greatly
struck by the reverent bearing and intelligent
look of the congregation. The boys and girls
from the school sang some hymns and songs
for us, the various parts being quite wonderfully rendered. One of the old Zulus who
was at the meeting had killed an ox in honour
of the Moderator's visit, and the flesh was to
be sold by auction for the benefit of the
church repair fund. Unfortunately we were

* While writing this volume I learned with very deep
regret that Mr. Matheson had died after a short illness.

only able to spend an hour and a quarter
at the mission, as it was absolutely necessary
that we should get over the first part of the
road before darkness fell. The homeward
trek was much more tedious, as the incessant
rain had made the roads worse, and at one
hill the car had to be backed many times
before it could be got out of a deep rut, and
even then the Moderator, Mr. Matheson and
I were all out in the mud pushing, helped by
some Zulus. Our average speed must have
been about five miles per hour, and even at
that the car was wagging like a dog's tail.
The last two hours were covered in black
darkness, and every few seconds would come
a jolt that almost sent us to the roof, so it
was with real joy and relief that at nine
o'clock we saw the lights of Glencoe, and were
soon rejoicing in the warmth of a real coal
fire. This was the first wet day there had
been for months, and rain was terribly needed,
but we did wish it had held off one day longer.
So ended our first visit to a mission station,
and we trusted all our discomfort was got
over in one big go, but this was a vain hope.

When we reached Durban a violent thunder
and rain storm was raging. Spite of weather

conditions, a large number of friends was on the platform to greet us, and we were driven to the hotel, where we found lovely flowers in our room; and every day during our stay in Durban fresh flowers were brought to me as a gift from the women in connection with the different churches.

" Resting near Durban " was how our printed itinerary described this period of our tour, and never was any sentence more misleading, because from the moment we stepped on to the platform at Durban station, until the day we left, every hour was filled with public or private duties, and the good people of Durban spoilt us with kindness. The only time I really felt to be my own was the forenoon hour I spent daily in the surf, and then in the magnificent swimming pond. I know this braced me up and gave me strength to withstand the rather moist heat of Durban in March.

From Durban we motored to Maritzburg by a very lovely road, passing through the Valley of a Thousand Hills. Over the weekend we were the guests of the Rev. Mr. Dewar, and had a busy time.

We left Maritzburg by train for Kokstad,

where we said good-bye to railway travelling, spending most of the next three weeks in motors, on roads defying description.

Our first visit in the Transkei (which is a tract of country lying, roughly, between Natal and Cape Colony, and larger than half of Scotland) was to the Mission at Gillespie. This was reached by car from Kokstad. The distance is about seventeen miles, and some idea of the condition of the roads may be gathered from the fact that Mr. Hunter, on his way to meet us, took seven hours to do the journey, once having to get the car pulled out of the mud by a span of oxen, while, on our return run we took four hours, and ran through a violent thunder-storm and cloud-burst, with roads at some places like rushing torrents over two feet deep. We stayed two days at Gillespie with Mr. and Mrs. Hunter, and greatly enjoyed their cheerful, energetic company. Various well-attended meetings of children, and of men and women, were held, and we had a warm welcome and received many native gifts.

Travelling during these three weeks was exceedingly hard and fatiguing. We commenced during the rains, which was bad enough, but when they ceased and the scorching sun hardened the clay into ruts many inches deep, the going was very painful in spite of air cushions, as the life of cars is a short one in that country, and often the springs were only memories.

Space forbids me mentioning in detail many interesting places visited, and many thrilling happenings. In every town or village meetings were held and as a rule I addressed large gatherings of women. The Moderator preached several times each Sunday and during the week, addressed meetings, visited colleges, schools, etc., and took part in several conferences in connection with the Presbyterian and also the Dutch Reformed Churches. Everywhere we met with enthusiasm and a welcome that was almost overwhelming.

One vivid impression received was of great friendliness and goodwill between the various denominations, and on nearly every platform one would find representatives from the Anglican, Dutch Reformed, Baptist and other Churches, and all uniting in sincere welcome to the Presbyterian Moderator.

There was great interest evinced in the (then) proposed union of our two Churches in

Scotland, and Dr. Morrison spoke on this subject everywhere.

I know how difficult it is to visualise a place you have never seen, but I wish you to try and imagine a very lovely but very lonely valley in South Africa, reached after leaving the main road, by five miles of a very rough track over moors. There are high hills on every side, and nestling on a plateau at the foot of the valley is the mission station of Sulenkama, with its tiny church three minutes' walk farther up the hill. No other house is in sight—the nearest white people are miles distant—only Kafir mud huts dotted here and there by hundreds.

The mission, a one-flatted house, with a deep veranda on all sides, is surrounded by large and beautiful trees, and to anyone going there for a visit seems a lovely and most desirable place, and so it is during the day in the glorious sunshine ; but oh ! the loneliness of it when the African night has fallen as it does so early in these tropical climes, and darkness, like a curtain, has drawn close around the mission house.

It is then one realises the isolation of the place, and appreciates the courage and bright spirits of these brave souls who have cut themselves off from home and all they hold most dear and dedicated their lives and gifts to the service of their heathen brethren. In all the mission homes we visited we never heard any talk of sacrifice or sense of love's labour lost ; rather an atmosphere of good cheer, wholesome fun and tremendous interest in all home matters, and no minister in any of our well-to-do home congregations takes more pride or pleasure in his pastoral visitation and congregational affairs than do these wonderful men, our missionaries.

At Sulenkama, Mr. and Mrs. Duncan Semple and their little boy and girl live, and there we spent two very happy, peaceful days. The Sabbath dawned brilliant and intensely hot, and even in the early morning we felt it very oppressive. At ten o'clock the children gathered for Sunday school, in the shade of a huge tree just opposite the house, and very picturesque they looked in their clean print frocks and overalls, the tiniest ones sitting on the ground in front. I was asked to take the address for the children, and spoke to them through a delightful native woman who understood English and interpreted very well.

The children sang some sweet Kafir hymns and solos, and Mr. Semple closed with prayer.

All morning, groups of natives had been gathering at the little church, coming from the hills and the valleys, many walking great distances. By noon, when our service began, so many were unable to get into the church that it was decided to hold it out of doors. Forms were carried out under the trees, and those who could not get seats were well content to sit on the warm, dry grass. During that simple service my thoughts flew away to another memorable out-door service, that Communion service held in Skye the year before. There in Skye, the Moderator stood in full Court dress speaking to a reverent, attentive congregation; here in Sulenkama, in the same dress, only in this case the congregation was composed entirely of coloured people. In Skye the heavens were grey, and a chill, damp wind blew which made sitting still a rather uncomfortable thing; here in Sulenkama the heat was intense, and no breath of air stirred. In Skye one heard the sound of the lark singing, the waves on the seashore breaking, and the bleating of sheep; in Sulenkama valley no sound disturbed the calm stillness except the speaker's voice, or a fervent " amen " as his discourse proceeded.

The natives are most reverent and interested as congregations, and do not fail to show their appreciation by audible responses. So different in environment, and character, and colour, and yet the same Lord and Saviour uniting us all, Whose love and sacrifice have made an unbreakable bond and Whose gospel is for the healing of all nations. All natives love music, especially singing, and it was inspiring to hear the great joyful sound of their hymns as it rose and swelled in the hot, still air.

At the close of the service the women all gathered round me, and I spoke to them and told them of the kind of work our women at home were doing and gave them a simple gospel message illustrated by a story. During this time the Moderator was addressing the elders, managers and leaders in the church, and at the close we were presented with addresses of welcome.

" When you cross the great river that has no bridge, we pray that God will swim beside you to the other side." Such was the quaint and, I consider, very beautiful message of farewell that awaited me on board the boat ere we sailed from Cape Town. It was sent by a branch of the Women's Association of the Bantu Church, and illustrates the practical and picturesque lessons the natives so often draw from Scripture. They had never seen the sea, and their widest stretch of imagination could only picture a great deep river to be crossed ; consequently there was need of God's protecting mercy. We came across many instances where, after speaking to natives, we found the seed had really fallen on prepared ground, and their simple, childlike nature and warm, receptive hearts made them most delightful to speak to.

My next memory is of a very simple, impressive Communion service held at another very lonely but wonderfully lovely station, Cunningham by name. We arrived there late one Saturday, as Dr. Morrison had been invited to take two services the following day. The church at Cunningham is one of the larger ones holding about one thousand people, but by eleven o'clock on the Sunday morning far more than that number had gathered, and throughout the service many stood outside the widely opened windows and doors. At the morning service the Moderator preached, the Rev. Mr. Ross, the minister, interpreting for him. After the sermon there was a solemn and very touching ceremony, when twenty-two young men and women were baptised and admitted into the membership of the Church. The Moderator, who was accompanied by an old native elder—who held the bowl containing the water—passed along the line, touching the brow of each young person with water, and pronouncing the words, " In the Name of Father, Son and Holy Ghost." After a dedicatory prayer and a hymn, the first part of the service was over. At two o'clock we again assembled, this time for the Communion service. The church was packed to its fullest capacity with communicants and many were obliged to sit in the passages on the floor. The Moderator preached from the words, " This do, in remembrance of Me," and after singing a hymn to our own well-known tune " Communion," the Sacrament was served.

Everything was done exactly as at home, the little morsels of bread, and the wine in large cups, and the Elements were carried round by the native elders. We were only a small company of five white people in a congregation of over a thousand natives, and yet it seemed the most natural thing in the world when I received the bread and wine from the hand of an old coloured elder. Is there anywhere except at the Lord's Table where coloured and white would sit down and eat together and feel no sense of incongruity. Truly the love of Christ is the great leveller of all racial and social distinctions. The feeling during that service was so tense, the spirit of true worship so manifest, one could almost feel the presence of the unseen Saviour as He passed up and down with joy amongst His kneeling people.

A third engagement, most interesting, and of an absolutely different type, followed. On account of the flooded state of the river we should have to cross to reach our next stopping place, we had to make a fifty-mile detour by an exceedingly rough but very lovely road. This was one of the hottest days we had yet experienced, and although we had two short rests on the way, we were exceedingly wearied when, at five o'clock, we reached Mbulu station. The scenery we passed through that day was grand—

moorland and mountain—and to get to Mbulu
we dropped 2,000 feet into a magnificent
valley, in which the mission house stands.
It is semi-tropical, and very hot most of the
year, but very lovely, and from the veranda
one has a view of gigantic crags and cliffs of
red sandstone which when caught by the
rays of the setting sun looked extraordinarily
beautiful. The vegetation was tropical and
many-hued birds flitted about.

After supper I went up to the little church
on the hill, just behind the manse, and there
addressed an audience of four hundred women,
who had been arriving in groups from many
distant parts all day long. Although only
7.30, the African darkness had long fallen,
and the church was only lighted dimly by a
few candles. I forgot my weariness and
every other worry in the interest and pleasure
of that quiet hour, and spoke and sang to
these dear simple people with gladness. No
outside sound disturbed us, and after the
simple service many of the women crowded
round me to shake hands and say " Thank
you." These native people are just like
children, very simple, affectionate and grateful, and after living amongst them for a few

weeks we quite understood why the missionaries became so attached to them, and love
their work among them.

Next morning dawned dull and misty,
and we feared might spoil the services, but
no! From early morn groups were arriving
to join the women who had slept in and
around the church. Then about nine o'clock
we heard distant sounds of singing and drums,
and gradually the teachers and children from
the schools in the valleys appeared, each
school headed by its own flag-bearer. The
Inspector-General had granted a holiday in
honour of the Moderator's visit, and when
the children's service began at ten o'clock
the church was packed. During this service
several of the schools gave quite excellent
exhibitions of chorus singing. Immediately
following this, there was a general service
which lasted till half-past one, and at the
close many speeches and presentations were
made. We walked the short distance back
to the mission house through dense crowds of
children and grown-up people, both Christian
and heathen, all singing their native hymns
as we passed.

After this there was feasting and rejoicing

s

on the hill-side for the rest of the day. Two oxen and twenty-two sheep had been killed and cooked in great pots out on the hill-side, and a crowd, which Mr. and Mrs. Auld estimated at thirteen hundred, squatted round the pots and fires and made merry. After lunch and just before we left we walked up and had a look at the unique and picturesque scene. As our car drove away several hundred women and children sang a farewell hymn, and even after we had taken our last look at the mission house we still heard the strains of that farewell.

After two hours' driving we reached and crossed the Kei River, where we said good-bye to Mr. Auld, and so ended our most interesting tour and work in the Transkei.

From this point I shall allow Dr. Morrison's Assembly Address to continue my story, only briefly mentioning one or two incidents and visits not touched by him. After leaving the Transkei with its great fascination but awful roads, we came to railways and really fine motoring conditions, and in our journeying stopped at King Williamstown, Grahamstown (that picturesque centre of education),

East London, where we spent Easter week-end, and then Port Elizabeth, our last halt before boarding the train for Cape Town.

We had a happy, full Sunday at Port Elizabeth, closing with a very large service in a huge picture-house at night. On Monday morning I addressed a splendid meeting of the Women's Association, before which tea was served; then at one o'clock we were the guests at luncheon of one of the Town Council. Fifty guests sat down, including the Mayor and Mayoress and ex-Mayor, and the lunch was served on the veranda of a restaurant just beside the world-famous " Snake Park," which we had time to visit before lunch was served. I would fain describe this gruesome but interesting place, where one can see within a small space about a thousand snakes of all sizes and species. It belongs to the municipality, and a great work is being done in collecting the poisons and the making of serums as antidotes for snake bites.

The journey to Cape Town *via* the garden route was a thing of sheer delight, the whole scenery being very beautiful; and at one

part, the " Montague Pass," the grandeur of
the mountains surpassed anything I have
ever seen. During those two nights we were
at a great altitude, and in the early mornings
the cold was intense, and made hot coffee
very welcome. The second morning we
arrived at Cape Town, where we were met by
our host (for the first few days), Mr. Reid,
Deputy-Mayor, and one of the best-known
and most highly honoured Scotsmen in Cape
Town.

During our ten days' stay in this interesting
and beautiful city, we had a really busy time ;
almost every hour was planned out for us,
and in addition to many church engagements,
we lunched on separate occasions with the
Governor-General, General Smuts, and
General Hertzog, all of whom we found most
gracious and interesting. There was a civic
reception in the Town Hall, a garden party,
and many other social functions.

Then there was a two days' visit to Stellenbosch, the seat of the Dutch University,
where the Moderator spoke at a Conference
of the Dutch Reformed Church. From
Stellenbosch one evening we drove by a
wild mountain pass to the little town of

Wellington, famous as the home of the saintly Rev. Andrew Murray. All these little Dutch towns are charming and full of interest and history, but space forbids any detail. The last day in Cape Town came all too soon. Good-byes had to be said, and on Friday, May 6th, after parting from a crowd of friends who had come on board laden with every kind of gift, we stood on deck with a real pain at our hearts, watching the outline of the beautiful Table Mountain growing dimmer and ever dimmer.

The homeward voyage was uneventful and pleasant, and at 6 a.m. on Monday, May 23rd, the *Edinburgh Castle* moved quietly alongside of the quay at Southampton. The same night at 10 p.m. we stepped out on the platform at Princes Street Station, Edinburgh, and had thus travelled over seventeen thousand miles and reached Edinburgh at the exact scheduled minute.

We returned to Scotland more convinced than ever of the infinite value of foreign missionary work, and of the abiding need of that work. Our missionaries and their wives are servants of whom the Church might well be proud. Overworked as they are, and

overshadowed by the fear that the Home
Church, in the interests of retrenchment,
may discountenance the continuance of the
white missionary, they yet give themselves to
their lonely work with a wholeheartedness
that is beyond all praise.

ASSEMBLY ADDRESS ON SOUTH AFRICAN TOUR

Dr. Morrison addressing the House, said :
" I was very unwilling to speak this evening, for I recognise that all the time on
this important occasion ought to be given
to the noble men and women who are actually
labouring on the mission field. But I am a
man under authority, and as I have just
returned this week from an extended tour
through our South African Mission Field, it
is regarded as fitting that I should say a
word. The tour was one of the most interesting and illuminating experiences of my
life, replete with incident, rich in splendid
fellowship, with moving accidents by flood
and field, and if I were ever tempted to doubt
the worth of foreign missions—and I do not
know that I ever was—I certainly never
could be so again. We began with the
missions in Natal and Zululand, and the

Assembly will be interested to hear that when I left Zululand, I was richer by one shilling. At the close of one of my sermons, a very handsome Zulu came to see me. He made a low obeisance, took my hand in both of his, and when he withdrew his hands I found in my palm, one shilling. There flashed through my mind a story I had once heard Principal Iverach tell of two negro preachers. ' Sambo,' said one to the other, ' how much did you get for your sermon yesterday ? ' ' I got one shilling, brother.' ' Sambo, that is mighty poor pay.' ' Yes, brother, but it was mighty poor preach.' I wondered for a moment if this was the smallest fee I had ever got, but I found I was mistaken. It seems that a Zulu is not allowed to enter the presence of his chief without an offering, and, as the native name for Moderator is the same as chieftain, this fine old clansman was bringing his offering to his chief.

" From Natal we entered the Transkei through Griqualand East—that interesting old republic of the half-breed—and as many people know nothing of the Transkei, I may in a word tell you what it is. The Transkei is a great tract of territory, more than half

the size of Scotland, stretching from Natal
in the north to Cape Colony in the south.
With the exception of one or two little towns,
and the traders, with their stations five miles
apart, and the missionaries, it is entirely
reserved for the natives. No Dutchman or
Englishman is allowed to buy land there,
and it is there, in that extraordinarily well-
governed country, that a great deal of our
mission work is done. We visited Gillespie,
where Mr. Hunter labours; and lone and
mysterious Sulenkama, scene of the labours
of Mr. Semple; and beautiful Rainy, where
Mr. Gavin carries on his consecrated ministry.
We visited Columba, the home for so many
years of that fine veteran, Mr. Auld; and
Blythswood, child of Lovedale, hive of industry, controlled into a perfect whole by
the organising genius of Dr. Stormont, a
man of whom the Church knows far too
little; and last, but not least, in a lonely
and isolated spot, not far from the home of
Christina Forsyth, in a tropical and snaky
valley surrounded by magnificent mountains,
we visited Mbulu, the home of that gallant
fellow, Mr. William Auld. I shall never
forget our visit to Mbulu. The women

gathered the day before, and Mrs. Morrison addressed them immediately on our arrival. They spent the night sometimes singing and sometimes sleeping in the church. The Inspector-General had given all the schools a holiday in honour of our visit, and early in the morning we watched the scholars coming down the mountain paths, some from five or ten miles away, each school with its banner and its drum, and before the morning was over, twelve or fifteen hundred adults had gathered. I was only a humble messenger of the Prince of Peace, but there could not have been more excitement if I had been the Prince of Wales. All the morning was spent preaching and speaking, and then in the afternoon there came the inevitable feasting. Twenty-two sheep and two oxen had been killed by the people, and it was very picturesque to see the cauldrons covering the hill-side, each with its own group round it. Crossing the noble River Kei, amid romantic Highland scenery, we passed into Cape Colony, and there at Emgwali, with its delightful Girls' School ; at Lovedale, which is too well known to require description ; and at Burnshill, for ever associated

with the name of that fine old chieftain,
Mr. Stewart, we saw what filled us with
admiration. Burnshill I could never forget.
The church, which held a thousand, was
crowded, and vast numbers could not get in.
I addressed the people and the elders, and
introduced young communicants, and, over
and above all that, I baptised thirty Kafir
babies. Mr. Lennox, of Lovedale, had come
over for the day, and I whispered to him
that I would like to take the babies in my
arms, just as I did at home, but that I feared
it would take too long. ' My dear fellow,' he
said, ' the longer you take here the more the
service will be appreciated.' It reminded
me in a flash of my own prehistoric days in
Caithness. I was sorry for these beautiful
babies. The mother passed them to the
father, and then the native pastor, eager to
have a share in things, made a grab at them,
and by the time they reached me they were
in a kind of shapeless mass of clothes and
bronze limbs. One look at my white face,
and the baby started howling, and the howl
was immediately taken up in sympathetic
chorus by the other twenty-nine. Talk of
community singing—it is nothing to com-

munity howling ! I believe I am one of the few men in the world who have ever heard thirty Kafir babies all howling at once. I baptised Nimrod. I baptised Hannibal. I baptised William Gladstone. I baptised Moderator. Some are born to greatness, and some have greatness thrust upon them. I baptised Morrison. Thinking that the last deserved some special attention I stooped down and kissed him—I call the baby ' him,' but I have not the least idea whether it was a ' him ' or a ' her.' Whereupon the interpreter, for the action was hidden by the upstanding parents, sprang on a seat and announced to the whole audience that the Moderator had kissed the baby. I think I preached pretty well among the natives, judging by the liberty I felt ; but that un-prepared and unpremeditated kiss was the most far-reaching sermon that I preached in Africa. There was no colour bar that day in Burnshill.

" Now, one or two impressions as I close, and first of all this. Sometimes on the trains, or on board ship, one heard slighting remarks about the missionaries, but I do not think I ever met a magistrate or a trader in the native territories who did not speak in terms of admiring approval of the missionary and his work. The Christian native is no more perfect than the early convert in the Church of Corinth. There are centuries of heathenism in his blood. But no one can mark the new expression that comes on to the face, the new refinement in the home, the eagerness to rise to a loftier morality than the old morality of the tribe, and the new passion for education so manifest wherever Christianity has come, without thanking God for the work which the missionaries are doing. The last thing I want to say is this. As many of you know, there is now in South Africa a native Presbyterian Church. It has its own Assembly and Moderator, its own constitution and procedure, and I think our Scots Church never did a wiser or a braver thing than when it entrusted such large powers of self-government to our native brethren. But if there is one conviction more profound than another with which I came away from South Africa, it is that that native infant Church, still uncertain of its steps, still dazzled a little by the light and liberty of Christ, still unversed in the great arts of government and of finance, is not yet able to stand alone. It needs, and it will need for a generation yet, the guiding and controlling hand of the European missionary, and to withdraw the missionary at this stage, and fill up vacancies with native pastors, say in the interests of financial retrenchment, would be one of the most tragic and disastrous blunders that a great Church ever made. I do not hesitate to say that in making this statement I am voicing the absolutely unanimous conviction of every man and woman in South Africa whose judgment is worth considering. I have talked with magistrates of the native territory, with missionaries of every communion. I have listened to speakers in native congregations, and received petitions as Moderator from native sessions, and without one single exception all are agreed in this, that to stop sending white missionaries now, at this particular stage in the evolution of the native Church, would be to imperil, and probably to wreck, the work of the past ninety years. I therefore beg the Church at home to see to it that no such policy is countenanced. The mere rumour of it is filling with discouragement every mission station in South Africa. And I beg some of our younger men who are eager for service in the foreign field to offer themselves for service in South Africa, one of the most fascinating and fruitful fields in the whole world."

DR. MORRISON'S VISIT TO THE SOUTH AFRICAN MISSION FIELD

By the Rev. Duncan Semple, of Sulenkama

The visit of Dr. Morrison to South Africa was an event of great significance for the African Christians who regarded themselves as belonging to Scotland. When it became known that the object of his visit was primarily to see the mission work of the United Free Church of Scotland, and to come into first-hand contact with the African Christians, their imagination was stirred to the depths. White Moderators many of them had seen, for the former United Presbyterian section of the Mission had been an integral part of the Presbyterian Church of South Africa for twenty-five years, and on a few occasions the Moderators had included the native churches in their official tours. And at long and rare intervals the mission field had been visited by deputies from Scotland who had been sent to investigate some phase of mission policy or to solve some delicate problem. But this was something entirely different. Dr. Morrison came not in his official capacity as Moderator, but rather as their " father " from Scotland, just to see his African children, to talk to them, to hear what they had to say and to see things through their eyes.

In a sense he came at the psychological moment. For many years there had been almost no recruits from Scotland for the widespread district work of the South African Mission Field. Almost half of the mission stations had become vacant inside a dozen years. Some of these were put in charge of young and inexperienced African pastors. In others temporary arrangements were made, and these usually consisted of superimposing a district on an already overburdened missionary. Many of the African Christians had begun to think that no more help was to be expected from Scotland, and there was a very considerable apprehension and uneasiness regarding the future of the Church if this state of affairs continued. " Scotland has forgotten us," was a common saying. " I-Skotland ixakekile " (" Scotland is too busy with its own affairs ") was on many a lip, and explanations of the dearth of ministers consequent on the Great War were unconvincing. It was into such an atmosphere that he came, and his coming brought relief to many troubled hearts. Scotland did care, after all. The Church to which they owed their birth had not forgotten them, for had not their great white father come himself to tell them so. It was as if a great paramount chief had gone far out of his way to visit and thereby to honour a remote, struggling and anxious tribe, and by so doing had brought them heart and hope.

What impressed the people was his graciousness and approachableness. Accustomed as they were to the regime of big chiefs and Government officials, they were prepared to behold an austere personage of commanding presence who from a fitting distance would speak to them weighty and memorable words. Had such been the case they would have considered it quite the proper thing for such an important person as the Moderator from

Scotland. They were not prepared for what they found—the quiet dignity combined with such a deep, warm kindliness in every word and action. They gazed in wonder at his smile, and went away with a new erectness. It did not matter who it was, man, woman or child, white or black. He made them feel that life was a great and a good thing, and that all it cost them was well worth while.

When the Prince of Wales was in South Africa one often heard the words, " The poor Prince." Day after day, sometimes night after night, the Prince had to appear before the public ; he had to speak, smile, bow and receive deputations and presentations. And one often heard the words, " Poor Dr. Morrison." Among the European churches and communities he had a heavy daily programme of addresses, receptions, luncheons and handshakings. When he came to the native territories the rainy season, which ought to have been over, continued with an aggravating persistency, and the rough earth roads, which were frequently raging torrents, must have meant torture to a delicate frame like his.

Yet he never pleaded fatigue or failed to keep an engagement, though many a time

T

flesh and blood must have cried out for rest.
Some ministers tried to protect him. On
one occasion, after a weary day, he was in
the vestry with the minister. A knock came
to the door. It was an old lady with a Highland name. She had never been to Scotland,
but her father had told her of the bens and
the glens, and she wished to speak to the
Moderator and shake his hand. The minister
told her he was tired, and could see nobody,
but Dr. Morrison had overheard the conversation. He went out, and brought her in,
and made her sit down and talk. On another
occasion he was discussing with a missionary
the itinerary of the following week, and when
he heard all that was involved he asked if it
could be done. The reply was that it could
be done by a strong young man, but that
after his long, harrowing journeys and num-
berless engagements it would be risky to undertake it. He thereupon decided to cut
out a certain difficult and arduous part of the
programme, and drafted a wire that was to
be sent the following day. But he slept over
it, and the wire was never sent. He carried
out all the programme, no matter what the
cost to himself.

The other thing that impressed the Africans was his addresses. It is not every learned divine from overseas that can speak in a manner easily understood by those simple and, for the most part, unlettered people. Many missionaries, at the outset, preach over the heads of the people, and their wise and earnest words fall far wide of the mark because they have not succeeded in putting themselves in the place of their hearers and looking at things through their eyes. Dr. Morrison did not make any such mistake. What was true of his Master was true of him. " They marvelled at the gracious words that proceeded out of his mouth " ; they marvelled that their great white father who was seeing them for the first time could speak the language of their needs and hopes so intimately and so closely, as if he knew where they had come from, where they stood, and where they were wistfully hoping to arrive. The time of the address was always a tense period. Whether the gathering was in the open air or in the church, it was always the same—a huge congregation, some on seats, some on the ground, some standing, but never a movement nor the rustle of a dress nor a cough, though many must have been aching owing to their crowded and cramped condition, every eye riveted on the speaker, so eager were they to catch every word. With their matchless memories they will recall and repeat his words for years to come. Already some of them are reading his books, and so universal is the appeal of the Gospel as presented by him, his written words also are finding their way to the hearts of the Africans as his spoken words did when they heard him face to face. The whole impression made by his visit to the South African Mission Churches is well summed up in the words of an old elder, "a more Christ-like man we have never seen."

OUR last summer holiday was spent in a delightful farm standing on a hill-side near Biggar in Lanarkshire, and the two months there were full of quiet, happy, and restful days.

The Doctor just loved the brightness and stir of the life about a farm, and took a deep interest in every detail pertaining to the work amongst the animals and also in the fields. He learned every term, technical and otherwise, in regard to agricultural work, and was storing his mind for future use.

He often said that all was grist that came to his mill, and during the winter his people in Wellington were fed with the finest of the wheat garnered during these summer days.

Looking back on these weeks at Biggar, I can remember noticing a distinct failing in his vigour, a disinclination to climb hills, and a shortening of our precious walks, but I tried to make myself believe that it was only due to the natural advance of years. All the same I was conscious that the time was drawing very near when he would require to slacken off considerably, and accept assistance in the work of the pulpit and pastorate. He had quite decided that if strength was granted him he would continue to minister in Wellington until the completion of his thirtieth year, and that he would then retire altogether. Many were the happy dreams we wove, and plans we made for the years we would spend quietly but busily together, because he always hoped to give much more time to writing when he retired, and in this way still carry on his ministry through his pen. However, God had other work and plans for him.

September was always an exceptionally busy month, and between our return from Biggar and the date of his last illness, he was immersed in the multitude of duties and arrangements dealing with preparation for the winter season's work. He attended in his usual methodical way to every detail, but afterwards I recalled how several times he had remarked, " I wonder why I get so easily tired, especially after my long holiday." I noticed his fatigue, but hoped it was probably due to his return to the less bracing air of the city. He visited among his own people until a few hours before he was obliged to give in and go to bed, and he must have carried on for several days although feeling very unfit. After his death I received various letters telling of visits paid during his last days to those not of his own congregation, and of his thought for others in the midst of his own weakness.

In almost every home or hospital in the city he was a loved and welcome visitor, and he did not confine his attention to his own patient only, but moved about the ward speaking friendly words, asking kindly questions, or playing with the children. One nurse said to me : " Some ministers come in and visit their own patient, and leave almost without anyone having noticed they were there, but Dr. Morrison always leaves everyone feeling happier and better." Only a short time before he left us, he had been visiting a church member in one of the infirmaries, and as he passed down the ward someone in a bed, who was a complete stranger, spoke to him. He waited with her for a short time, learning her trouble and circumstances, and prayed with her. When he was leaving she said : " I am to be operated on on Friday at 12.30, and nobody really cares whether I live or die." " Oh, you must not say that," replied the Doctor, " I care." And on the morning of her operation she received a little note saying, " I shall be thinking of you at half-past twelve." By such constant deeds of loving thoughtfulness his path was strewn up till the very end.

The day before his last illness he visited all afternoon and received callers all evening, and I know that one visit paid was to a girl— an absolute stranger—who had been brought to his notice by someone in church. At that house he left flowers, and the memory of a kindly, interested visitor, although his state of exhaustion was apparent even to strangers.

Among letters received was the following :

" It was only an everyday occurrence—a ring from the door-bell—but often in the common things of everyday life the unexpected happens. On opening the door I found standing on our door-mat one who had been for many years my favourite preacher and writer, Dr. George H. Morrison. I immediately asked him indoors. He complied with my wishes—though he seemed a bit bewildered.

'But, why should you ask me in?' he questioned,
'do I know you?' 'No,' was my reply, 'but then
I know you; in fact, everyone knows Dr. Morrison
of Wellington.'

"He seemed tired that day, so I asked him to
sit down and rest for a little; he did so, and we
talked together. One can understand how pleased
I was to have such an opportunity, I who had
envied others that great privilege. How natural
he was! His wonderful personality seemed immediately to set one at ease, and one found oneself
talking to him as if to an old friend.

"I do not think he was feeling well even then—
for he spoke of growing old; mentioning that before
going to visit anyone living on the top flat, he
always inquired at one of the houses downstairs if
he were quite correct about the number, etc. 'You
see,' he added, 'these stairs seem to tire me so.'
Here, then, was the reason why my distinguished
visitor had called that day. Having received the
desired information, he departed with these words—
'Be sure and give me a big smile next time you
see me.'

"Next day I received a post card with these
words written in the Doctor's own beautiful hand-
writing:

"'Thank you so much for your kindly welcome
yesterday. These little things warm one's heart.
'G. H. M. 28.ix.28.'

"Need I say how delighted I was that he should
remember me—but, little did I know then that in a
few short weeks he would be gone, and that I

should not see my new friend again. But his post card remains one of my treasured possessions, and carries with it a fragrant memory of one who lived a devoted life."

This visit was among the last he paid, and tells of his failing strength, but unfaltering courage and thoughtfulness.

One has written :

" The year that has now elapsed has revealed to many—more and more each week in its passing— how much we owe to the beloved minister, who by his preaching, by the example of his consecrated life, and by his wonderful gift of friendship, made our lives deeper and infinitely richer. While he was here with us I feel as if we took so much that was wonderful just for granted and now when the gracious presence has been withdrawn, and the tender, sympathetic voice is stilled, we begin to realise with an ache of loneliness how great is the blank in our lives.

" For myself these twenty-six years of his ministry have been a time of continual inspiration, and many more must have had the experience that the unseen foundations of things were being made more real to them year by year under his ministry. More and more one felt his life and teaching were one, and that in this unity was to be found his enduring power to attract all kinds of people to his message. Silently but steadily he was preparing men in mind and heart for that revival of religion he so earnestly desired and so confidently looked for, and, when it comes, those who follow him will without difficulty trace his influence in its beginnings."

Although he did not go as he often said he hoped he would, at his work, there was no long illness, no weakening of his intellectual power, just a short ten days in bed, during which time he was able, in spite of much discomfort, to read, and up to the day before his going take a keen interest in everything concerning his work and people.

The night before he died, he dictated some notes to his secretary, and spoke hopefully of getting away for a change, and then returning to work more fit than he had been for years. Next day, Saturday, 13th of October, after a rather restless night, a severe and unlooked for hæmorrhage occurred, and in spite of the skill and wonderful attention of three doctors and a surgeon, he passed quietly home.

His trust and hope had always been such realities, that death held no terrors for him, only the surety of a new beginning, a passing into a larger room. He knew that when the Call came he would not have to go down into the Valley, or cross the River alone, but that his Saviour would meet him on this side, and be his Guide and Comforter.

Very shortly before the end, he turned to the nurse and said, " It's an ever-open door, never closed to anyone. It's wide open now, and I'm going through."

Then with a scarcely perceptible sigh, and eyes wide open as if seeing already the glory beyond, he passed into that land where is fullness of joy and knowledge. I am convinced that already there was stealing on his ear the distant triumph song, and that he knew he was being watched for by those who had already arrived. His whole life was such a witness to his living faith in a fuller existence beyond, that one could not but share in his certain hope and joy. The very last sermon he preached was two nights before his illness. Speaking to a large audience of Sunday school teachers and leaders of other organisations for the young in Gorbals Church, " he took for his text two phrases from the fourteenth chapter of John : ' I will love him, and will manifest myself to him . . . we will come unto him, and make our abode with him.' What was felt most of all was the spiritual power of the preacher. The audience, composed mainly of young people, listened in almost breathless silence while he quietly and persuasively reiterated his four points : ' I will love you,' ' I will manifest myself to you,' ' I will come unto you,' ' I will abide with you,' until they seemed indelibly impressed on every heart and mind. Towards the close he said, ' This winter none of us knows what will happen, but—there is this promise of His : " I will abide with you." Looking back on the experience now, those present feel as if they could never forget the shining face of the preacher or the haunting cadence of his voice as he seemed to lift them up into a more serene atmosphere of faith."*

Remembering his love of bright colours, and in response to his own statement, " I shall welcome flowers," very few white wreaths were sent, and at the funeral service the massed beauty of rich colouring in front of the organ and surrounding the coffin, which rested in the Choir, softened the sense of sadness and separation, and made one feel how he himself would have gloried in the wealth of beauty. The crimson flowers on the coffin symbolised triumphant hope.

---

* From newspaper article by Mr. Alexander Gammie.

" I lay in dust life's glory dead,
And from the ground there blossoms red,
Life that shall endless be."

The whole musical service struck a note
of triumph and completion. The praise
chosen was the 23rd Psalm, and his favourite
hymn, " There is a land of pure delight."
There was no Funeral March at the close of
the service, but by request Mr. Turner played
" Crossing the Bar," and surely it was never
played more magnificently or with more
vibrant soulfulness. When after the quiet
opening bars the hymn swelled into its
gloriously triumphant ending, one felt that
the player was indeed inspired by the occasion, and the thrill that passed through the
great audience could almost be felt. Even
those who do not claim to be musical said
afterwards that they were simply carried
upwards by the beauty and triumph of the
playing.

One of his favourite illustrations was of
how he loved to stand on the Roman Wall
in Hillfoot Cemetery, and look across to the
rugged line of the beautiful Campsie Fells,
and surely no more fitting place could have
been chosen for his long rest than that peace-

ful spot close to the Roman Wall, where the wind blows ever fresh and free, and where it seems that at every season of the year the larks are singing. His thoughtfulness for others was expressed in the desire that the service at Hillfoot should be brief, and that the mourners should not remove their hats.

He disliked intensely the wearing of deep mourning or, indeed, of black at all. Especially did he dislike the way in which degrees of sorrow were expressed in clothes, and often said to me, " I hope you won't wear black long if I go first, because to my mind it is quite wrong, if I have gone, as we believe, to a better and brighter home."

No, he wanted to be remembered as one living in happiness ; even greater happiness than he had ever known (and in spite of many dark hours, and much physical oppression, he was a happy, contented man). He often said, " I believe in a Saviour Who knew how to smile, and Who loves to see His children happy."

Among the appreciations, one has touchingly and truly written : " Only to the mortal shell of the beloved pastor and preacher have the congregation bade farewell. His work and influence will shine on radiantly, a life-long inspiration to his hearers and his successors. I have never seen a gathering more deeply moved, and yet I am sure there were few tears. As I left the building, and watched the silent crowds, and carriage after carriage full of glowing flowers, I understood then what Maeterlinck meant when he said, ' There is no death.' Dr. Morrison has but passed on into the higher service of the Master to Whom he dedicated all his great powers of brain and heart and soul."

"Some of us fall out by the way, and some go to their sleeping chamber before others, but we shall all meet in the gladness of the morning ; and none will be waiting with a sweeter welcome than the man who learnt here, that death is but a shadow in the way, and life's fullness is not here, but yonder."

A REMEMBRANCE BY DR. J. STUART HOLDEN

One of the abiding memories of life, right on to the end, must be that of my service at Wellington Church, Glasgow, during the last week of Dr. Morrison's life. He had been accustomed year by year to invite some brother-minister in whose work he took pleasure—and never was there a man of his eminence as preacher and pastor who so wholeheartedly appreciated the efforts, often poor enough indeed, of men lesser than himself—to conduct special services preliminary to the Communion Sabbath in October which inaugurated the winter's work in the congregation. Such invitations were always regarded by those who received them as a high privilege. To have secured the confidence and to share the friendship of George Morrison was honour enough to humble any man the while he prized and endeavoured to be worthy of it. I never knew of any one of us who declined the invitation if it were humanly possible to serve our friend.

Prior to my journey I knew nothing of his more than ordinarily threatened condition of health. It was a great shock to be met at the Central station with the news of his breakdown the day before, and of the doctor's embargo upon any visitors. With characteristic thoughtfulness he contrived to send me a personal message of affection and confidence, bidding me carry on the special services as arranged, assuring me that though laid aside, he was really present with the flock he loved,

U

and entrusting me with a word of greeting to them. There was no thought of anything but of his recovery and return in the mind of any ; and throughout the week no cloud of the coming storm of sorrow dimmed the fellowship of an uniquely united people. Day by day I was able to encourage them with the tidings they wanted most to have— of gaining strength and what appeared to be well-founded hope. And a spirit of grateful praise expressed itself in every gathering.

It had been his purpose to receive into Church-membership, upon their profession of faith, some thirty young men and women on the Friday evening, when the service was specially designed as a preparation for the coming Communion Sabbath. My suggestion that this should be deferred until the next Communion season, so that those who had come to know the Saviour through his ministry might have the joy of being welcomed to His Table by their own loved minister, he would not entertain. Although such an event always marked for him one of the really high days of his ministry he laid this sacred privilege upon me, sending me the questions he was accustomed to put to the candidates, bidding me give the right hand of fellowship in his name, and rejoicing in the evidence of the real unity of all believers declared by one of another branch of Christ's Church acting in such a capacity at Wellington. At the same time he begged me also to preside at the Communion Service which he had himself expected, as always, to conduct. And the welcome news accompanied the request that the doctors considered his progress sufficient to warrant the giving of their permission that I should visit him on the Sabbath.

He was, however, to hear tidings more direct than those I should have brought him. For Eternal Love had already decreed that he should actually be present at the Sacred Feast, one of " spirits of just men made perfect," holding fellowship with those who worship on this side the Veil. For after an entirely unexpected collapse which took everyone by surprise, he passed over in the early Sabbath morning, " and all the trumpets sounded for him on the other side."

All unaware of what had happened the great congregation assembled for the Communion Service, to be informed by stricken office-bearers who kept the doors, of the translation of their leader. It was a people dazed and benumbed that filled every seat in the building, the eyes of all irresistibly drawn toward the seat behind the spread Table, so peculiarly and fittingly his own, which he would never again occupy. Could it be true ? The Kirk Session, a fine body, including some of Glasgow's leading citizens, each one of them his leal friend and brother were as men crushed and undone. To be admitted to a share of the grief that bowed them as we met to consider the situation, and the course it called for, was a sacred experience. By common consent it was decided to observe the Sacrament for which the people had gathered and thereafter to suspend all services until after the interment. And together we went into the church as men who had already drunk of the Cup and been baptised anew in the Cloud.

For myself, and I doubt not for many, that Communion Service can never be forgotten. It was as though we had met on Heaven's threshold—as indeed we had. And the glory that shone through the Open Gate by which he had gone in transfigured the tears that were on every cheek. At once, in few and simple words, I told his people all there was to tell, and tried also to pay my own tribute of grateful affection to one who was my loved friend—the first of many such to be rendered publicly during the coming week. Then with full hearts we sang, and there was a thrill of Christian certitude and triumph in every line beyond anything I ever realised.

> How bright those glorious spirits shine,
> Whence all their white array ?
> How came they to the blissful seats
> Of everlasting day ?
> Lo ! These are they from suffering great
> Who came to realms of light,
> And in the Blood of Christ have washed
> Those robes which shine so bright !

Dr. Morrison had developed in the course of the years at Wellington an order of Communion Service which emphasised in turn its varied aspects of Thankful Remembrance, Spiritual Fellowship, Joyful Hope and Grateful Consecration. And it was, on that memorable morning, faithfully followed. In a silence that could be felt, broken only by a suppressed sob here and there, the elders carried the Bread and the Wine to the waiting people, upwards of thirteen hundred receiving the Sacred Symbols. Throughout there was an undertone of the undying joy that sorrow, however deep, cannot invade. For Christ Himself was in the midst, and the sense of His presence was an uplifting reassurance which entirely banished gloom. Such a service, held under such circumstances, was one of the most powerful evidences of the reality of the Faith, and of the quality also of the ministry under which that company of disciples had been built up in it. Fittingly it closed, just as he who was in all thoughts and memories had ordained it should, just as Communion Services under his guidance had always closed, by the singing, to " Boswell " of that paraphrase of the Master's word which runs :

> Let not your hearts with anxious thoughts
> Be troubled or dismayed ;
> But trust in Providence divine,
> And trust My gracious aid.

Surely never can they have been sung with a more general and thankful sense of their aptness to the happenings of that ever-to-be-remembered Sabbath. And surely never did

a congregation go out from the Table of the
Lord with hearts more thankful to Him for
the gift of such an under-shepherd as Dr.
Morrison had been to them, or with firmer
determination to "follow the Lamb whither-
soever He goeth" even as he did. For myself, I turned from his pulpit and his vestry
as from holy ground, to cherish for all time
the privilege of having, by his magnanimous
affection, shared with him, in even so small
measure as is all I could ever hope to do, the
privilege of a ministry which was always
redolent of "myrrh and aloes and cassia out
of the ivory palaces." He left his mark on
many men. Not least on him to whom fell
the honour of presiding, in his first absence,
at the Table from whence, in his Master's
name, he was wont to dispense His gifts with
such winsome grace that it was as though
He were Himself at the head of His board.
And the mark he left was one of the marks
of the Lord Jesus.

UNIVERSALITY OF HIS APPEAL

Much has already been said and written
in regard to the universality of Dr. Morrison's
appeal through voice and pen, but I feel that

it might be of interest if I append a few letters and notes which illustrate this side of the Doctor's work.

EXTRACT FROM MINUTE OF STATUTORY HALF-YEARLY MEETING OF GENERAL COUNCIL OF THE UNIVERSITY OF GLASGOW

HELD WITHIN THE BUTE HALL ON WEDNESDAY, OCTOBER 31ST, 1928

DEATH OF THE VERY REV. GEORGE H. MORRISON

On the motion of the Convenor of the Business Committee, J. C. Scott, Esq., M.A., seconded by the Rev. John Fairley Daly, B.D., and supported by the Chairman, it was resolved that the Council should place on record its sense of the loss sustained by the death on October 14th, 1928, of the Very Rev. George H. Morrison, M.A., D.D., who was a graduate in Arts of this University, and in 1913 received from his Alma Mater the honorary degree of Doctor of Divinity, in recognition of the fruitful outcome of his scholarship in his unusual achievements as preacher and pastor.

In 1926 his Church, in token of the esteem in which he was held for his own and for his work's sake, called him to the chair of Moderator of the General Assembly of the United Free Church of Scotland.

His ministries in Thurso and Dundee were a presage of that long period of noble service as minister of Wellington Church, Glasgow, where for

more than twenty-five years he so laboured that
there gathered about him in constant affection one
of the largest congregations in Scotland. He attained a remarkable popularity as a preacher and
teacher. His expositions of the great verities of
the Christian faith were so simple, and touched
with so charming a literary grace, that their depth
and the secret of their calm might escape the un-
discerning ; for he had, in an almost superlative
degree, the gift of transforming seemingly remote
doctrines into living and vivid counsels for the ways
and problems of daily life. His books and periodical
articles extended his message throughout the
English-speaking world, and thousands who had
never heard that silvern and winsome voice of his,
were everywhere directed by him in green pastures
and beside still waters. Of set purpose he almost
limited his activities to the opportunities of in-
fluencing his generation which his pulpit afforded.
But this definition of his work gave it an intensity
and a power of quiet and persistent appeal which
marked him out as one of the greatest Gospellers of
our day.

Eric Liddell, the champion runner of
Olympic fame, one evening occupied the
pulpit in Wellington Church, and gave an
address to a crowded audience of men. He
writes :

" DEAR MRS. MORRISON,
" The *British Weekly* has just lately arrived
telling us about the Doctor's Home Going. The

news was so sudden that we could hardly believe it.
Week by week we have enjoyed the pieces he gave
to the world, and Mother was just saying that when
on furlough next we must spend some time in
Glasgow, if for no other reason than that we might
go to Wellington Church and hear him.

" This will just be one of the many notes of
sympathy in your bereavement, but it comes from
one, I might say that it comes from a whole family,
who feel that they have lost a friend, and one who
has inspired them all. He lives again in the lives
made more beautiful by his life. We thank you
for all he has meant to us and pray that in this
time of sorrow God's richest peace may be with you.

> " Yours very sincerely,
> " Eric H. Liddell."

" Tientsin, N. China."

From Dr. Lauchlan MacLean Watt, Glasgow
Cathedral :

" To have known Dr. George Morrison is to have
enriched the abiding memories enshrined within our
hearts.

" The very thought of him is pleasant, for he
carried with him a quiet as if of enfolding wings,
and he communicated the spell of it to you. You
felt that very specially in your sorrow. The great
grief of my life came to me not long before he was
taken home : and I do not remember what he did
or said, but I know that he comforted me. It was
because he walked clothed in faith : and his heart
was love's own lantern. The dark was touched with

a new light when he came into it ; and the resurrection promise seemed more sure.   Yet he was not a solemn personality, he had every human gift. His words could glint with humour, he loved to laugh.

" I never wondered that his people loved him to the edge of worship, for he had the universal touch. No poor man could help forgetting his poverty, and no rich man his wealth when George Morrison touched them.   Both alike felt that they had come into contact with one whose heart carried a greater treasure than the Bank.   He had the truly religious gift—that is, he did not speak religion to you, but he made you feel that religion must mean just that which gave significance to his personality.   He was even in his silence an eloquent witness to goodness and the graces of the highest life.

" A man like him dies always before his time— that is to say, the world can never spare them. Men feel a constant ache of loss when they recall the thought of him.   Yet a man like him dies always at his fulness ; having lived every day in the light of God, he is ready and ripe for the divine ingathering.

" I miss him out of my daily walk but never out of my daily thought.   His personality was so quietly pervasive that I should not be astonished were I to meet him when I turn the corner of the street familiar to us both.   And when we meet hereafter it will be just as when we met here, for in him there was no intervening ' No Man's Land ' between earth and heaven.   He did not need to hoist his sail when he turned homeward, for he was always moving

before the breath of God.   He had only to set his
helm for the rising sun.

" I never say good-bye to souls like his.   I only
try to press on after them, and hope they may not
win too far ahead for us to overtake them and
resume the comradeship broken meantime here."

The Archbishop of Rupert's Land, on Dr. G. H. Morrison :

To the Editor of *The British Weekly*.

" Sir,—May I from overseas and far away venture
to send a tribute to the late Dr. G. H. Morrison ?
I never had the pleasure of meeting him personally,
but all the same I had learned to look upon him
as a warm and inspiring friend.   *The British Weekly*
will not seem the same to me without his charmingly
helpful weekly sermons.   Winsome in their beautiful simplicity and bringing new and fresh meanings
out of familiar texts, they yet revealed a depth of
profound learning underneath, which gripped those
who read them.   Though, as I have already stated,
I had never the privilege of meeting the dear man,
yet I felt somehow that I knew him as a friend—
a humble man of God, possessed of a singularly
alert mind which lent a charm and a grace to
whatever he wrote.   ' God's gentleness had made
him great.'   I cannot refrain from paying this
tribute to a man who was a ' succourer of many
and of myself also,' though in a far-off land.

" S. P. MATHESON (Archbishop).

" Bishop's Court, Winnipeg, Manitoba,
   " November 13th, 1928."

" Cape Town,
" January 11th, 1929.

" DEAR MRS. MORRISON,

" Your kind note has arrived, also the book, with its memories of a happy hour spent with you and Dr. Morrison. Little I thought then that we should never meet again. I thank you for the book, which I shall read with deep interest. You have a great memory to cherish. And as we get older, life more and more comes to consist of memories—and the Great Hope.

" With all good wishes,
" Yours ever sincerely,
" (General) U. SMUTS."

" The Hirsel,
" Coldstream.

" DEAR MRS. MORRISON,

" I am not worthy to write these few words, for so many enjoyed a far longer friendship with Dr. Morrison. You know the feeling of safety and assurance of reaching one's destination when one listens to the regular throb of the engines and turn of the screw as the ship drives its way through a storm.

" It was that sort of feeling which Dr. Morrison inspired.

" You have told me that the Doctor insisted on solitude in the morning, unless a visitor or the telephone brought an urgent message. It may well be that his obedience to the order, ' Be still and know that I am God,' was the direct cause of his power to strengthen, encourage and cheer others.

He seemed to say to one, ' I have thought, and thought, and thought again, every difficulty has been faced, every question answered, every argument examined, and at the end of it all, the truth of the words, " Lo, I am with you alway " is the certain conviction of my life.'

" He somehow conveyed the true meaning of a certain faith, a certain hope, a certain trust. With him beside us we would have felt quite safe in the storm of life, and assured of reaching our destination. Without him we are not so confident, but far more so than if we had not known him.

" Perhaps people like Dr. Morrison are not allowed to be with us too long, or we would only be passengers and not navigators of our own boats. We will never forget that he showed us the course to steer, and how to weather the storms, and before he left us called out, ' Be of good cheer. All's well.'

" Yours sincerely,
" HOME."

THE END